Hildebrand's Travel Guide
SEYCHELLES

Publisher
K+G, KARTO+GRAFIK Verlagsgesellschaft mbH
© All rights reserved by
K+G, KARTO+GRAFIK Verlagsgesellschaft mbH
Schönberger Weg 15–17
6000 Frankfurt/Main 90
Third Edition 1987
Printed in West Germany
ISBN 3-88989-069-5

Distributed in the United Kingdom by
Harrap Columbus,
19–23 Ludgate Hill,
London EC4M 7PD
Tel: 01 248 6444

Distributed in the United States by
HUNTER Publishing Inc.,
300 Raritan Center Parkway,
Edison, New Jersey 08818
Tel: 201 225 1900

Authors
Impressions: Wolfgang Debelius, Christine Hedegaard, CJ Eicke
Facts: Clausjürgen Eicke,
Christine Hedegaard

Photo Credits
Clausjürgen Eicke, Dieter Lampe,
Christine Henze, Jürgen W. Laupert,
Helmut Debelius/IKAN, Reinhard Scheiblich/IKAN

Illustrations
Eckart Müller, Peter Rank, Manfed Rup

Maps
K+G, KARTO+GRAFIK Verlagsgesellschaft mbH

Translation
Helmut Taylor

Lithography
PPWS, Lorenz, 6000 Frankfurt/Main 70
Haußmann-Repro, 6100 Darmstadt
Spandau Repro, 6500 Mainz-Finthen

Type Setting
LibroSatz, 6239 Kriftel

Printed by
Schmitt+Läufer, 6300 Gießen

Hildebrand's Travel Guide

Impressions
Photographs
Travel Experiences and Reflections

Information
Land and People
Your Travel Destination from A to Z
Useful Information
Contents

Supplement: Travel Map

Captions

1. One of the capital city of Victoria's most prominent features and, in a way, its trade mark: the "Clock Tower", constructed (along the lines of the original in London's Vauxhall Bridge Road) in 1903, when the Seychelles first became a British Crown Colony.

2. Examples of houses built in the traditional style, with palm leaf roofs – as here on the western coast road by Barbarons– can still be found today in the more remote areas. The occupants value the efficient "ventilation" and the screening effect against the sun and heat.

3. White settlers and Negro slaves "laid the foundations" for today's racial mixture in which all possible shades of skin colour, ranging from white through "coffee" and "chocolate" brown to black are represented. The exotic accent lent by the admixture of Indian and Asiatic influences, are reflected. And they all, not just the children, do live peaceably together, irrespective of skin colour.

4.–6. They are known as the "Seychellois", and that's also how they describe themselves. There is, in fact, talk of a self confident "new race". Let it suffice to say that, in the Seychelles, one encounters a breed of man such as is found nowhere else on earth – the description does the rare beauty of the Seychelles women justice too!

7/8. Victoria market on a Saturday morning. It's a social occasion, good for a chat as well as the place to buy your fruit, vegetables and any of a variety of goods offered for sale. The Seychellois are a gregarious, talkative folk; their Creole tongue a pleasant-sounding relative of French. Gaiety is no stranger to these parts.

9. A good walk to the nearest stream has often to be taken into account since piped water is still a luxury in some parts. For the Seychellois, "cleanliness" is certainly "next to godliness."

10. Along the St. Louis River, off Bel Air Road, only a few hundred yards from Revolution Avenue, Victoria, you find one of the favourite washing (laundry) spots. The laundry is beaten clean on rounded flat rocks and then dried in the sun on boulders; an exchange of local and family news is part and parcel of washday.

11. Fish is the islanders' principal source of dietary protein and, together with rice and breadfruit, constitutes their staple diet. Their fishing boats are usually between 15 ft. to 30 ft. long, modest in size, and the catch they bring in from the coastal waters – as here at Beau Vallon Bay – will normally just about cover their personal needs, leaving a few over for sale.

12. The local way of bundling up fish for sale: a palm thong threaded through mouth and gills. 15 to 20 fishes can easily be carried to market in each hand; the customer needn't worry about carrier bags – he carts them home in the same way.

13. Traffic, on La Digue, is the same today as it was years ago. Apart from a few pick-ups (for supply purposes), cars are still banned. He who desires to be transported has to make do with the oxcart – this includes the baggage-laden tourist. It certainly doesn't pose any environmental hazards and is a most sedate mode of travel. Alternative means of achieving locomotion along the mostly narrow and palm-lined island lanes: the bicycle or Shank's pony.

14. In order to "ride" the surf on the reef, you need a fair sized boat – 30 ft. to 40 ft. – and an adequate crew.

15./16. The multitude of brightly coloured ocean fauna is a marvellous sight for both the snorkler and diver. In the Seychelles waters you find hundreds of different sorts of fish. Above (15) an emperor snail, below a flame goby (16).

17. A stretch of Seychelles beach – straight out of a picture book: fine white sand is sifted by the shimmering, rolling turquoise sea and flanked by granite cliffs and waving palms – a clear, deep blue sky completes the picture. Although it might sound like a cliché, it's the truth, the whole truth and nothing but the truth, as the beaches at Anse Intendance (Mahé), Grand Anse (La Digue), Anse Lazio (Praslin) and many others will verify.

18.+21. The Seychelles' most famous botanical rarity – complete with its fruit – the coco-de-mer. This palm does not reach its full height of in excess of 130 ft. until it is about 800–1,000 years old; the fruit achieves its full weight of about 30–40 pounds after about seven years. Apart from a few examples growing on the island of Curieuse and in the botanical garden on Mahé (our picture), Praslin (which has about 4,000 of these palms) is the only place on earth where they grow.

19.+20. The abundant variety of indigenous Seychelles flora, much of which is exclusive to these islands, is unique in its diversity and does the description "exotic tropical splendour" more than justice. Our two examples: tropical hanging hibiscus (19), and blackeyed Susan (20).

22.–25. Symbolic of the so-called granite islands of the Seychelles: is the charming way in which the sea and the wooded heights, interspersed with grey or pinktinged rock, complement one another. A variety of magnificently different views gladden the eye: Anse Takamaka/South Mahé (22); view over Victoria harbour, from Belvedere (23); the normally calm waters of Anse á la Mouche (24) and the – from time to time – rougher waters of Port Glaud Bay (25), both on the west coast.

26. Anse Volbert, on Praslin: one of the longest, widest, and most beautiful beaches of these granite islands. The water is shallow up to the reef, but the sea still remains crystal clear in the deep waters beyond; at low tide and when there is no wind (as here in our picture, taken in May), it's so still and warm that you could imagine you were in a giant bathtub.

27. Bird Island (our picture) and Denis Island are the only coral islands and they can be reached by 'plane from Mahé in about 30–40 mins. This is a real dream of an island, lined with white coral beaches, covered with palms and casuarien trees – and home to a unique colony of sea birds.

28. In the period April/May to October/November, millions of sooty terns come to breed and rear their young on Bird Island. The air is full of their cries and the sky overhead sometimes dark because of the mass of flying birds. The breeding grounds take up about $\frac{1}{3}$rd of the island.

29. It's a hard fight for the best breeding spots on this hard, treeless part of Bird Island. Where all goes well, the family consists of parents and just one egg – which hopefully will hatch into...

30. Permanent inhabitants of Bird Island are these fairy terns which are beautiful to behold and elegant in flight. They share the island with the common tern, the barred ground dove and the Madagascar fody as well as with two giant tortoises and furthermore with the island's owner and the staff necessary to attend to the wants of the maximum 50 visitors who are accomodated in Bird Island's palm-thatched bungalows.

31. Sundown over the Seychelles: a fairy-tale experience. This view is of Beau Vallon Bay, showing the silhouette of Silhouette Island on the horizon.

They Go by the Name of: The Seychellois

You just can't help liking the people of the Seychelles. One might even envy them a little: because of the terrific climate which they can enjoy here; because of the abundant tropical vegetation which provides them, without their having to do much for it, with the essentials at least – coconuts and fruit, fish and vegetables – and because of their carefree and lighthearted approach to life, which is more in tune with today than tomorrow or the next day.

A sight one sees so often, never tires of and which allows an inner smile: with a bundle of fish tied together with a palm thong, his straw hat set at a jaunty angle on his head, a Seychellois strolling home in the midday heat. The faded T-shirt proclaims "Thank God it's Friday", but that's just by the way: today is a Monday.

People are never in a hurry in the Seychelles, especially when on foot (it's sometimes a different kettle of fish when motorised) and even the various modern-day influences have not seduced them away from their traditional lifestyle, a style of life characterized by a certain happy-go-lucky, well – lethargy.

The language itself, Creole – a homely, melodic exercise in phonetics – gives expression to their carefree, even phlegmatic nature.

The European normally finds all these sorts of things very strange at first. But only, usually, for about the first three days. Then he suddenly finds the atmosphere definitely bearable, even soothing. One automatically begins to take things more easily than at home, to slow down and enjoy life; the fact that Nature, which surrounds you, comes close to our idea of paradise, helps a lot too.

To look at, the Seychellois differ somewhat from island folk such as those of the Caribbean. Many of

them are dark and have essentially Eurasian facial features. Often the list of descendents will include Africans, Indians and Asiatics. However, the European influence is not to be denied – this has been the English and French settlers' contribution in helping to create this unique racial mixture of the Seychelles (some go so far as to talk of them as a "new" race).

The young women and girls are unquestionably good looking. Someone, sometime and somewhere summed it up well and in a most original fashion, when he described their spiritual and physical qualities in this way: "French enough to have a good figure; English enough to be well-behaved; Asian enough to possess that hint of the exotic; African enough to harbour the call of the wild". Needless to say, this doesn't only apply to the girls here, but also to their male counterparts.

The children are a particular joy to behold. Always neat, clean and tidy, it is a real joy to see the hundreds of colourfully dressed young children swarming out of school, on their way home at midday.

A good half of the Seychelles population is, by the way, under 25. The working people go about their daily business in shops, hotels, in various government ministries or in the agricultural sector which has, of late, been successfully developed. The lot of staying at home and forming the core of what is, from our point of view, an "expanded" family unit, falls to the grandparents.

(Hedegaard)

The Seychelles – And that Quip about the "1,000 Miles"

Well, it certainly went down in history, that remark once made by one of the Seychelles' British governors, when he described the location of the islands as "a thousand miles outside the world". He wasn't altogether wrong either, if Africa is taken to mean the then known world. They do in fact, lie about 1,850 Km east of Mombasa, in Kenya, which distance is more or less 1,000 nautical miles. Looked at in another way, one could laud that govenor's sense of humour in circumscribing the phrase "off the beaten track". The heart of the matter, taking today's perspective into account, would tend to be that what in those days might have been interpreted as banishment is, today, in contrast, rather something to write home about: being sent to one of todays' most desirable tourist locations.

Small wonder it is then, that capital has been made out of this amusing "blast from the past": "Unique, by a thousand miles", shows the poetic licence that the tourist media has allowed itself in interpreting that historic statement.Under this banner the islands hope to steer successfully into the future after having experienced a number of lean years.

And the funny thing about it is that one can't fault these poetic banner wavers as, quite frankly, the claims they make for their islands, do without a doubt, hold good not only for a thousand miles in any direction, but on a far wider stage as well – the world. Where else on this earth do you get a group of granite islands slap bang in the middle of the ocean? Where else do you find such wide and sweeping, or hidden away and intimate little fine sandy beaches nestling in the shelter of imposing granite cliffs? The answer of course is on the Seychelles; the inimitable, unique Seychelles.

There's plenty more to astound you, don't worry – there are quite a few things here you'd have real trouble finding anywhere else. For instance, the islands are a veritable "Noah's Ark" of nature: a wealth of zoological and botanical species has been able to develop and evolve unhindered over millions of years on these "out of the way islands", and is still there, for us to observe. For example: flourishing exclusively on the Seychelles islands of Praslin and Curieuse are the fabled, double-cheeked coco-de-mer, which were once thought to grow on the bottom of the sea. And this is just one of the 80 varieties of plants which grow exclusively on the Seychelles. There are 13 varieties of land-birds which draw scientists and hobby ornithologists from the world over, because they are no longer to be found anywhere else. These include the black paradise flycatcher, which was once feared extinct but has now successfully bred on a reserve on La Digue.

Let's refer to the above mentioned famous 1,000 miles once more: that is about the greatest distance you could travel within the Seychelles archipelago, which, in that seemingly endless expanse of the Indian Ocean, encompasses an area of something like 160,000 sq. miles – an area which would include Germany, the Benelux countries (Belgium, Holland and Luxemburg) and Austria. If you add the actual surface area of all the (around 100) islands together, then you still only end up with a figure of about 160 sq. miles, i. e. about twice the size of Greater London. Quite extraordinay, the relationship between landmass and sea area, at 1 : 1,000 – wouldn't you say?

Mr. Grimshaw and the Ghosts of Moyenne

Moyenne, with its encircling belt of fine white sandy beach and shallow waters, lies in the middle of the Seychelles Marine National Park – and is one of the smaller offshore islands lying off the capital city of Victoria. You can get there by scheduled boat service, from Victoria, in about 20 minutes. At the jetty, on arrival here, you'll be met by a jolly Englishman, Brendan Grimshaw, who has a good tale or two to tell the small groups of guests which come to visit his domain. According to this island proprietor's accounts, "there's a pirates' ransom buried in these parts". And, in truth, historical documents (papers date back two centuries) indicate that there are two graves on this island, in which treasure is buried. The absolute authenticity of the claim may, however, be in some doubt. The redoubtable Mr. Grimshaw himself is in no doubt and maintains that speculation about the credibility of the claim has grown in recent years. Adding fuel to the fire, in 1974 a young lady on Mahé dreamed that the two treasure-bearing graves were located next to a mango tree. The young lady had never been on Moyenne, and in consequence her vision was not taken all that seriously but it transpired, after period of heavy rainfall which caused a certain amount of topsoil subsidence, that a further gravestone was laid bare, exactly at the spot she had seen in her dream!

Whilst on a tour of the islands, you might have the good fortune of having Mr. Grimshaw relate the rather frightening account of how, as he began in earnest to search for the treasure and had just begun to dig for it under a coconut tree, he was nearly brained by two falling, beautiful specimens of coconut. He says that was enough for him, and he gave up the dig. Mysterious too, is that a divining rod will dip at exactly the spot where he was digging, as well as at another spot at which he suspects treasure to be buried. Strange, strange.

He's got a few more stories up his sleeve as well. Stories which tell of rattling windows, slamming doors and call images of the supernatural to his listeners' mind and the goose pimples out on their flesh. It's all good stuff though. The route round the island is, in parts, clad in flitting shadows and passes two old ruins. One of these, known as "The Doghouse", was originally built by an Englishwoman, as a dogs' home. She lived on this island from 1899 to 1919 and cared for homeless animals.

The pathway comes to an end at a now completely restored old Creole villa, at which visitors can rest on the shady veranda. A long, cool beer or a refreshing drink of coconut milk does you a power of good at this stage. To cap the day's exitement, the view from here into the mountains of Mahé and onto the turquoise blue waters of the Marine National Park, takes your breath away. *(Hedegaard)*

Highlights

You can read the words "Bus Stop" stencilled in the sort of lettering you'd expect to find on a wooden packing case, on a simple wooden sign on the roadside, where the bus to Mahé is supposed to stop. One can only imagine that a certain prospective passenger didn't find the red lettering on its white background sufficiently colourful and perhaps, in an idle moment, thought that a visual aid was required. Our sign had been embellished with the drawing of a comical-looking green bus with black wheels and a white running-board. Fun and games, before we've even started! Traces of the old lorries, in which the lucky passenger was transported on wooden seats, are only to be found in the scrapyards nowadays. To suggest that one of the tourists – normally only to be seen in the airy mini-mokes or in taxis – takes a public bus, is to risk the proverbial raised eyebrow. Enough of airy thoughts and back to the order of the day, which, in a bus here, means, chatting with your neighbour. You'd think you were in another world – overboard is where you can throw those polite notions from back home, of keeping yourself to yourself whilst getting from A to B. The scene here is much more casual, colourful and friendly, and the gaily-dressed impromptu crew of paying passengers are willing and unstilted conversationalists. You get a fair sprinkling of old ladies in broad-brimmed straw hats, laden down with the day's purchase of farm-produce. There's a young mother with her two charming and well behaved young daughters, one of whom is shyly proffering the fare to the conductor. The girls have pigtails tied with what might have been silk ribbons but are, in fact, simply strips of coloured cloth – cut, presumably, from a garment no longer serviceable. They're sweet, gaily dressed and every bit clean, neat and tidy. Opposite is an old man – or does he only look that way because his hands are rough and his face lined and weatherbeaten from the sun? He too sports the commonly seen straw hat – in contrast to several of the younger generation, sitting nearby, who advertise their commitment to today's "cool" world in that they sport trendy jeans, snazzy shirts and the much sought-after quartz wristwatches. One of them has got a briefcase – I wonder what's in it and where he's going to – another is engaged in a seemingly highly-amusing conversation with the bus driver whose attention is thereby more than perfunctorily diverted from the unforeseen hazards these narrow roads might at any time place in our way; my blood pressure rises a little. My immediate neighbour, posing the regulation questions put to all tourists, enquires as to my name, where I come from and how I like it on the Seychelles and starts – without dwelling too long on my actual response – to chat with me freely and openly. He tells me that he has gotten himself a job as a lorry driver after having been unemployed for some time; that he is quite pleased about developments but that money is in short supply – as everywhere – and that prices are high. He's looking forward to getting married soon and shows me a picture of his intended who works in a shop in Victoria; together they expect to get by quite nicely. I warm to my refreshingly sincere travelling companion, who reminds me that this is exactly how all of the people in the Seychelles are. And this is probably the most lasting impression one takes home from the Seychelles: how the people here may be seen to treat each other in such a friendly and natural way, show genuine interest in other people and are completely free of agression.

In the Vallée de Mai, on Praslin, you could well imagine that you had mysteriously been transported back into a prehistoric age. Only the carefully laid out paths (equally painstakingly kept clean by ladies wearing the – almost – obligatory Seychelles hats) betray the fact that human hands have been (and are) at work here, to make the homeland of the fabled coco-de-mer accessible to the visitor.

You need walk only a few yards from the parking-lot to find yourself in the middle of a green palm thicket in a scene so playfully punctuated by the myriad and changing hues taken on by the shafts of sunlight piercing the folliage from above. The leaves of young coco-de-mer palms, still seedlings, in fact, grow up and outwards from the ground, in the shape of giant fans several yards across. No wonder that the locals put them to good practical use: as such to thatch their roofs; woven as screens, room dividers (macoutis), or all-purpose baskets (kapatias). Coming off the older palms which have developed trunks, are fan-shaped, long stemmed leaves which stretch out towards the skies but bend under their own weight, down towards the ground. The adult specimens, varying between 70 ft. to in excess of 100 ft., wave slowly and pensively to and fro in the wind, like metronomes under the weight of their ample, multiple fruit stems which will normally hold between 3 and 5, but can carry as many as 10 of these "twin" coconuts of varying sizes, meaning a total weight of anything from 200 pounds to 400 pounds. The dull thud of one of these ripe "monster" 20 to 40 pound fruits coming to rest on the soft ground – covered by a layer of dead, fallen leaves – is frightening, to say the least. By staying on the pathways one avoids any possible danger of being "crowned" – the ripened, potential hazards are removed in time. The male palms are rare enough for you to have to search for them – apart from the one standing like a demonstration model at the entrance. The long, piston-like seed panicles normally issue forth from the base of a dense outcrop of branches about halfway up the palm, and dangle downwards under their own weight. In nature's scheme of things, the green gecko is often to be seen climbing about amongst the orange coloured blossoms and could, consequently, be described as a "fertilisation agent" for the female palm.

And, before you ask, yes, there are other types of palms to be seen as well. For instance: the Vallée de Mai has some vacoas – "corkscrew palms" – which have only a relatively thin trunk and are easily recognisable because of the bizarre stilt roots on which they stand, and the way in which they and the profusion of leaves corkscrew – hence the name – sunwards. Here and there the palmiste palm has got its roots dug in; they grow to over 100 ft., are sort of slim-line specimens and the grateful connoisseur's donor of that sought-after "millionaires" salad, palm hearts – they're taken from the trunk of the palm. The ordinary everyday coconut palm lives here too, but they, again, are pretty few and far between. Looking upwards, you'll see that the leaves of this multitude of palms form a pretty effective foliage roof under which an eerie stillness reigns supreme when the wind has dropped. Then, when a sudden gust of wind comes along, the silence is broken by the sound of the far outstretched coco-de-mer leaves bashing together. That too can be a frightening moment to the newcomer; the sound is more than startling, and reminiscent of two corrugated iron sheets being smacked together. Above that sort of din you don't expect to hear the chirping of those of our feathered friends which live here – and you don't. Truthfully though, the sounds made by the interesting bird-life in these parts are better described as "calls". Bird watcher or not, be warned that the Seychelles vasa parrot is such a messy eater, that he's in the habit of dropping (apart from other matter) titbits of his meal from his perch high above you. Let "Lady Luck" smile on you this day and the droppings fall just a little downwind, because being granted a sighting of this (more darkgrey to brown coloured) "black parrot" or his mate – they like to live in small groups – is tantamount to being favoured amongst men. To put it another way: many of the Seychellois themselves will have lain in wait, in vain, for a glimpse of this, one of the rarest of this world's birds.

Sunset over the Seychelles
That red glow gracing the heavens, after the sun has dropped below the horizon, is the same throughout the tropics. It's the little "extras" which delight the senses, lift the heart – and of these the Seychelles has a surfeit to offer.

Is an island rising out of the ocean an impressive sight? One could mention Silhouette first – could it have been named thus to give expression to the spectaculer view its outline presents, as seen in the dying sun, from Beau Vallon Bay? Or, take the islands of Cousin and Cousine, which, from Grande Anse, on Praslin – sometimes showing great banks of cloud towering above them – will present you with an unforgettable, wistful and romantic picture. Then there's La Digue, with its already pink-tinged granite cliffs that will start to glow like the dying embers of a fire in the soft evening sunlight.

And on Mahé: yours the sweet sensation of contentment as – in the view from La Misère – the gold-red heavens darken, the harbour lights come on and Victoria prepares to greet the falling night.

Perhaps the most memorable experience: sunset over Bird Island. The sun will hardly have dipped below the horizon before, suddenly, thousands upon thousands of the island's sea birds will have taken to the air, to scour the ocean for food. Their shrill, haunting cries fill the air as they perform the most amazing manoeuvres in flight, plummeting vertically down into the waters then rising into the skies again – whilst the ocean's waves, breaking incessantly on the even, white sandy beach, beat out a rhythmic accompaniment. Dotted with soft white clouds now highlighted by the sun's last rays, the spreading red fire of the evening sky is darkned more and more by the multitude of soaring birds. One thinks, fleetingly, of "Hitchcock's" thriller, "The Birds", but the awe-inspiring majesty of this, nature's spectacle, brooks no comparison. And, as the mantle of darkness gently clothes the shimmering white sands, should reflection pay emotion's reverie court, be it in acknowledgement of nature's grace in having allowed this marvel to unfold before one.

"Island Hopping"
There will be those amongst you who treat boarding an intercontinental jetliner with the same respect as entering a lift. Others, there again, will have found pleasure in travelling less distant routes. "Island hopping" will – no matter which category of traveller you fall into – prove an exhilarating experience. With a little luck, you could be sitting there next to the pilot, watching his every move and marvelling at all the instruments and dials.

Just the fact that you're sitting there in the immediate vicinity of the pilot, gives "island hopping" an atmosphere of friendly familiarity – and the trim 9–17 seater "Islanders" and "Trislanders" (that's what the white-painted Air Seychelles craft are called) do the rest. And not only camera-toting tourists take advantage of this mode of travel to get from island to island. You get mothers with children, on their way, possibly, to see a specialist on Mahé; a grandmother, on her way to visit a relative; businessmen carrying important-looking briefcases; a mechanic who's been called out for a repair job somewhere – and so on.

All of the passengers, now sitting 2 abreast down the length of the cabin, had to undergo a most remarkable procedure at the airport in Mahé: each one, as well as his baggage, had to be weighed! The point being that every spare pound of payload can be used to carry necessary goods – parcels, newspapers, magazines, spare parts etc. outwards, parcel, fruit and bird's eggs etc. on the return journey. Even the flight announcement, just before starting up, was tinged with originality. The pilot turned briefly to face his passengers, and said: "Morning – Air Seychelles – Praslin – no smoking, please (points to sign) – safety instructions (he holds the card up high) – O.K.? – Let's go". And we did.

Almost all of the passengers are looking down out of the windows excitedly. Cruising height is usually around the 1,000 ft. mark and you can, therefore, not only see things, but you can also clearly recognise them. Little fishing boats tracing a thin foamy wake in the turquoise ocean, islands floating on the water – all can easily be picked out and you can even see the palm trees. The islands have an almost unbroken girdle of white sandy beach; around some you can even see what appears like a thin silver halo – the waves breaking on the surrounding coral reefs! And there, as the pilot points out, banking the 'plane a little so that we get a better view, a school of dolphins playing, easily clearing the water every now and again and hurrying on their way. On the horizon great banks of cloud are stacked up on top of one another, contrasting sharply with the deep blue of the skies. Immediately prior to our landing approach we nose through some clouds ourselves; the little 'plane shudders. Finally – we're almost down – I can clearly discern the island's narrow coastal strip of light-coloured sand with its palm trees and little, seemingly toy houses which get bigger with every passing second. And now, bump, we do touch down on the short airstrip; one can hardly tell it apart from the green of the airfield. Cut engines; doors open: "Welcome". "Island hopping" is great!

– P.S.: under the heading of "Island Hopping" come not only hops by 'plane, but also island to island travel by boat, schooner or ferry.

To "pop along" to the **market quarter of Victoria,** is to both look and find without end, to have one's legs refuse to propel one along at anything faster than strolling pace and for one's head to reel under the influence of a multiplicity of colourful impressions and memories. That market scene there, by the fruit stall, looks just as though it had been plucked out of Cabbage Row, in Gershwin's opera, "Porgy and Bess". That old colonial building across the way, with the wrought-iron balcony, isn't that just a "doggon" piece of New Orleans? And this alley here, with its higgledy-piggledy assortment of crooked corrugated iron huts: such bright shades of turquoise combined so boldly with raspberry reds and forcefull yellows are, surely, otherwise only to be witnessed in the Caribbean? Over there, shops bearing signs saying "General Merchants", looking as though they could grace the pages of an ancient picture book und whose proprietors turn out to be messrs. "Leong Thiong" and "S.R.K. Naiken", respectively, are so jam packed with goods as to remind one of Chinatown in Singapore; the bewildering assortment of aromas issuing forth assaults the senses and brings images of an Indian bazaar to mind. The name under which this market is known, is – in genuine English – wait for it: "Sir Selwyn-Clarke Market".

All this and the people – in whom the either African, Indian, Asian or European heritage, in varying combination, is clearly mirrored – reflect not only the Seychelles' historical past but also the present day situation. The hustle and bustle of trade: in order to sell them from their stalls, men carry three or four bundles of fish in each hand; women, stroll about under that giant mango tree in the centre of the market, carefully comparing the prices of oranges, salads, aubergines or cassava roots; children, to whom some kind trader has given a stick of sugar cane as a lollipop; mothers who procure a modest weekend joint for their large families in the narrow arcade of butchers shops; men, who for a few rupees have the tobacconist weigh out their weekend ration of "smokes" from his big green tobacco chest. A thoughtful pause: a chat here, a friendly word for an old acquaintance there.

It's difficult to tear yourself away from this scene which is not, in any way, put on for tourists, but is – life itself. Life as it is elsewhere only seldom, and in a few years possibly nowhere else to be experienced.

Victoria, the World's smallest Capital

There are plenty of capital cities where the visitor always feels that he is under some kind of obligation to keep on the move – whether it be running a sort of cultural "gauntlet" or being caught up in the maelstrom of entertainment and shopping. But that is not Victoria!

This little capital city (and with no more than 25,000 inhabitants one may be excused for using the diminutive) is a pleasure to behold: easily finding one's bearings, the town presents the (hectic) European with a refreshingly different, charming, leisurely and colourful experience. The Seychellois from "the sticks", on the other hand, tend to come away impressed by the pace of it all. And sure, the rhythm of day-to-day life does seem faster here than on the rest of the islands. It's certainly true of the market (Market Street), with its friendly atmosphere, where fish and meat, fruit and vegetables, town-gossip and spices are turned over in quantity. They can be pretty sharp, these Seychellois, when it comes to haggling over the price of a tasty bit of fish or the cost of papaya. And, as the seasons and the harvests change, so does the selection of available produce vary. In the narrow streets leading to the market, Indian and Chinese shopkeepers offer a wide selection of, principally, cotton garments for sale. Colourful and multi-coloured cottons are the locals' delight. The visitor from Europe will find this picturesque scene captivating.

A shopping spree in the streets around the Clock Tower is fun. A stone's throw from the Clock Tower – which resembles Big Ben – are the shops of Independence Street, Rachel Street, Albert Street and those opposite Victoria House. If you haven't already got your "Bou Bou" – a multi-purpose piece of cotton material available in a variety of colours and patterns – this will be the place to get one, as well as some bargains in cotton beachwear.

Opposite the main post office in Independence Road, souvenir shops offer a selection of chic articles, jewellery and some kitsch – sea shells, dolls and basketwork, coco-de-mer in both actual size and miniature facsimilies – but brown and well-polished, for sure. Next door, in the "Home Industries Store", the selection is wider, the atmosphere more tasteful and the prices hardly higher. At times when one prefers to sit down and rest, have either an iced-drink or hot coffee and watch the people strolling by, the café of the famous "Pirates Arms" hotel is the place to go. This is where people congregate to see and be seen, to hold a friendly conversation with the person – male or female – adjacent or to do a quick bit of business.

Not more than a few yards away you get a crash-course in the marvels of modern architecture: a great, grey box-like affair with an immense, reflective glass front, as anonymous and cold as the dealers of financial destinies it conceals; the yellow building next door, is Independence House in which, amongst others, the Seychelles Tourist Board, the News Bureau and the Tourist Information Bureau are located, the latter being the source of all useful and necessary information for the tourist. All newly built, as is the elegant monument on the roundabout in front of them: a modern-day counterpart of the nostalgia of the Clock Tower at the other end of the road.

On the way back in the direction of the old town, the National Museum is worth a visit. The various and extensive collections provide an excellent overview of the Seychelles' history. The Stone of Possession, erected on Mahé by the French, in 1756, is also on view. The natural history of the islands isn't forgotten, and the museum exhibits sea shells, examples of coral and, of course, the coco-de-mer.

If, when you come out of the museum, you can't find a taxi outside, then turn right at the Clock Tower, and there, opposite St. Paul's Cathedral, you'll find the main taxi stand. Should you prefer to take the bus home, then continue walking up Albert Street and turn right into Palm Street where nowadays, opposite Unity House, all the buses stop. You can get a bus in any direction from here – including to your hotel. The clock on the Roman Catholic cathedral rings out the hour (when the mechanism functions) in a remarkable way: once on the hour, and again two minutes later. Should you find yourself in the vicinity, when the hour is full, lend an ear. The theory has been put forward that the time is "tolled" twice in order to assure the ruminative and dilatory Seychellois of another crack at getting it right.

Michael Adams the Painter

"To Mr. Adams, please." Before it sinks in that you haven't had to say which Mr. Adams or where he lives, the taxi will have gotten smoothly on its way. The fact that Michael Adams is a well-known personage here might, so far, have escaped your attention, but the unerring way in which the taxi driver makes his way to your stated destination, at the mere mention of his name, soon makes it quite clear. If the taxi driver knows the place so well, he must often take people there. And the more often he takes people there, you might muse, the more famous Michael Adams would be…

And you're not disappointed. He is constantly in demand, and the only chance of an uninterrupted conversation with him is by arrangement, during the early evening, before he retires to his 13′ x 13′ "jungle studio", to do what he loves best – to paint, listening to classical baroque music.

As hardly anyone else before him, he has aspired to "capture" the Seychelles on canvas. And that he has been so unmistakeably successful in this is borne out by the fact that his name has become the "brand name" of the Seychelles – even though he was born in Malaysia and lived for a good many years in Uganda, East Africa. It is the very fact that exhibitions of his works have proclamed his artistry – thereby also the Seychelles – to the four corners of the world, that prompts the admission that doing a little more in this respect is a question of time as well as financial means. In fact, he prefers people to come to him and, indeed, counts famous actors, racing drivers and prominent politicians and businessmen as well as nobility, amongst his patrons.

Michael Adams – lively character that he is – gives the impression of being a settled man. Not least of all his childhood experiences allow him to describe himself as a "forest and jungle man". As his pictures deal principally with the forest and jungle around and about his house which is built in the old Seychelloise style, one could say that he's got his model "sitting" right outside the front door. Green and yellow applied with that inimitable brush stroke give his pictures a certain lightness, against which his use of brown introduces a contrapuntal note, an earthiness, which, in his view, is an essential element of the jungle. In alluding to the six dimensions of his paintings, he means that all six senses should be stimulated by them, that one should see and hear and smell the jungle in them.

He increasingly often includes people, unmistakeably Seychellois, in his paintings, forging a compositional link between them, their rural or urban environment and the immediate natural surroundings. To find inspiration for his paintings, he will, for example, sit in his car opposite a bus stop, observe the people and their continually changing movements as they wait, and draw and sketch.

He finds the title of "Gauguin of the Seychelles", which a German newspaper once conferred upon him, amusing rather than touching. His pictures and their style, he himself and his family are living proof of the fact that the contrary is true. The question of isolation from the outside world, or of leading an "alternative" life style, does not arise for anybody in this family – they lead their own lives here.

If – without the assistance of an obliging taxi driver – you would like to visit Michael Adams, then head for the south-western portion of Mahé. You'll find his house hidden in the trees, about 20 yds. off the coastal road, in the middle of the woods near Baie Lazare Village. But don't worry, a large sign at the driveway to his house, saying Michael Adams Paintings, will tell you you've arrived. Of course you can purchase what takes your fancy – the selection of available motifs and formats is wide, the price range hardly less so.

Underwater Sports in the Seychelles

The Seychelles lie just about in the middle of the Indian Ocean, far, far away from the great continents with their polluted coastlines. I'm just a little sceptical, however, as all the various places that I've visited to go diving at in the tropics have had much in common. Will the Seychelles prove any different?

The jetliner shudders, just a little, in the turbulence during the landing approach; the sky is overcast; the islands below are a sorry looking sight – dark outlines in a steel grey sea; and I can see rain clouds hanging like shrouds about the mountain tops. We land without incident on Mahé, principal island of the Seychelles archipelago, and the diving instructor from the Aquanaut Diving Base, on La Digue, is there in the reception hall to greet us. He makes light of the situation: "It doesn't often rain for more than 14 days in a row here". I have to laugh – in a pained sort of way. That's exactly how long we'll be staying for! We effect the transfer into something resembling a bus, and we're off in the direction of the harbour, past rain-drenched locals and some amazing and impressive looking lush vegetation. To my left a bare cliff-face reaches up into the clouded sky, and, to my right the ocean swells. From the harbour we begin the last leg of our journey: 4 hours by boat, to La Digue and I begin to "feel" the proximity of the islands. And then suddenly a glimmer of red cuts through the mantle of colourless sky: the sun's back! I can see that even the diving instructor is breathing a sigh of relief. The fantastic fireworks of colour in the sky take my breath away, as does the spectacle of the sun setting, crowned by three different rainbows.

A dinghy comes out to pick us up, A last dance with the waves, a jump, and you're home and dry. Then a beer, a bungalow and a bed. Outside the jungle is alive with noise. Morning is heralded by the sound of driving rain; the noise made by the shower unit hardly merits the description "driving"; breakfast is of ham 'n' eggs and all's well with the world. Our diving gear is loaded onto an ox-cart and we trundle off in the direction of the harbour to the "La Feline", Aquanaut's motor yacht. We motor round the island and I'm actually well-impressed by the view. The combination of imposing granite cliffs and palm trees is really exceptional especially so now, as the sun is back. Confusion reigns as people change. But, no matter – splash, the water is crystal clear and the mighty cliff faces seem to have followed us below the water. The now happy group of divers quickly disperses, and I have time to take stock: there are many differences between here and the Maldives for instance. Here one doesn't seem to get the profusion of coral growth which is so typical of the atolls. The hidey-holes that fishes need are, nevertheless, plentiful; cracks in the rock, little niches, great fissures, caves and hollows and overhangs etc. And in and amongst all these various hide-outs you get all the fascinating swimmers such as demoiselles, turtles and cuttlefish and more or less completely hidden away in their lairs, crabs and crawfish. Knowing the different types of fish there are, I can tell the distinct African influence here. For instance, coral beauty and wrasse of this colouring are otherwise only to be seen in Kenyan waters. Underwater visibility is good and constant at about 60 ft.; the water is warm and only a mild current felt. An absolute dream of a dive, especially for a photographer.

On the reefs you need to keep a wary eye out for the prickly and plentiful sea urchins. The stiff drink you need, in order to bear the discomfort or having the spines extracted from various parts of your anatomy, is small comfort indeed. That said, it's also true that this sort of experience is about the most dangerous that might befall you, because the potentially dangerous deep-sea sharks hardly ever stray into the shallow waters of the Seychelles Plateau. The maximum depth of water around the islands is about 230 ft. but we seldom dived any deeper than 90 ft., simply because that was "rock" (excuse the pun) bottom.

Excursion to the "Good Ship Ennerdale"

The programme offered by the diving centre includes two sorties daily, from La Digue, to different diving spots, and the maximum of one hour's travelling time involved lets you get a good sunbathe in on deck.

One of the high-spots of a diving holiday in the Seychelles has "gotta" be a descent to the "Ennerdale", a giant tanker which went down off

Mahé, in 1969. Thanks to the fact that it had already discharged its cargo of oil, the question of pollution did not arise. The British Navy blasted the sunken wreck apart, nicely separating "fore" and "aft". And so, in depths varying from 25 ft. to 100 ft., you'll find a ship's torso to do the flights of fancy of even the most demanding "wreck fan" justice. Great shoals of mackerel are constantly going through their paces around the top of the wreck; in the wreck itself, parties of bat fish, resembling mourners at a funeral, hover about with expressionless eyes, observing their unfamiliar visitors; moray eels have made the tanks – now ripped open – their home, and the gangways, pipes and stop-cocks are overgrown with coral sponges in all colours of the rainbow. One of the divers poses comically on one of the toilets in the crew's quarters, and another mimmicks the pilot, on what's left of the now blown-up bridge. The actual guardian of the wreck is a rather capital grouper, which has grown to a magnificent size and is a real "divers delight" to see. The wealth and variety of fish-life to be seen here is genuinely impressive and we decide to pay the wreck another visit, despite the several hour's journey involved in getting here and back again.

Excursion to Cocos Island
You just cannot afford to miss the fairy-tale bay of Grande Anse, on La Digue, with its fantastic white powder-sand beach and forest of palm trees fronting sheer, smooth granite cliff faces. Or Cocos Island, which we sailed to from the African Safari Club's Paradise Hotel, on Praslin. We dropped anchor off Cocos in less than an hour and, kitted out with just the bare snorkelling essentials, we had the proverbial "ball". In the shallows, where the water is about 6 to 8 feet deep, the underwater scene is knock-out. Here, but only in the waters sheltered by the island, you find lush coral beds. We are just floating on the surface of the water, and can see 50 yards or more through our diving masks! A quick dive below the surface attracts the little clown fish, who rush immediately towards the intruding, supposed feeding rival. Their hosts sport violet-coloured mantels and deep yellow tentacles. At one fathom the light coloured sand still reflects the rays of the glistening midday sun strongly enough to dazzle your eyes. But there's better still to come; as though out of nowhere, a giant shoal of powder blue surgeon fish comes swimming towards us. The mass of blue-coloured fish is in continuous motion. Flitting about, they nibble at the algae growing on the branches of the outcrops of coral, and take little or no heed of the other snorkel divers as they approach. It's a sight which fascinates us all. Brightly speckled parrot fish accompany us on our swim to the shore.

Cocos Island itself turns out to be the true paradise island: it's out of the way, different from the rest and you can experience the pleasure of discovery in an almost out-of-this-world combination of cliffs, sand and palm trees.

(Debelius)

Coco-de-Mer, the Fruit that came out of the Sea

The well-travelled seafarers of yore were astonished: what manner of strangely shaped fruit might this be? And where did the locals get them from?

The fact that one would find them washed up on the beach provided a sort of clue, but a clue which only served to shroud the question of their origin in even more mystery. Everywhere, where they were washed ashore – on the eastern coasts of India and Ceylon, the Maldives and even Indonesia – that self-same question, "where on earth do they come from?", could only be answered by a quizzical raising of the eyebrows. One of the legends as to their origin told that they could only be the fruit of a giant underwater tree, and this tale served to give the double-cheeked nut its name: coco-de-mer.

The allusion to femininity which its smoothly rounded, double-cheeked shape allows, has resulted in the belief that the coco-de-mer possesses some very special properties – above all, those of being an aphrodisiac and of a cure-all for the aches and pains of old age. These attributes and the fact that the coco-de-mer was pretty scarce anyway, made it into a highly-prized, expensive, rare collectors item; even the crowned heads of Europe were caught in its spell. It is reported that Rudolf II of Habsburg, emperor of the Holy Roman Empire, acquired one of these nuts shortly before his death, in Prague, in 1612, for the tidy sum of 4,000 gold ducats. A princely sum indeed, for which some 5,000 dairy cows would, in those days, have changed hands. His court jeweller, Anton Schweinberger, embellished it with gold, fashioning it into an ornate drinking vessel which

can still be admired in the Museum of Historical Art, in Vienna. Also housed in Vienna, in the treasure chamber of the "Deutsche Orden", is a most artistically worked example of coco-de-mer. Further exhibits may be found in the British Museum, in London; in the "Grüne Gewölbe", Dresden, East Germany; in the University of Uppsala, and in the Provincial Overijssels Museum, in Zwolle, Holland. Other, decidedly more profane uses of the nut have been reported. The halved, hollowed out nut is used by the fisherman of the Seychelles and Mauritius to bale out their boats, and – so the story goes – as a begging bowl, in Calcutta.

The cloak of mystery surrounding the "fruit that came out of the sea", and the status it had enjoyed as an exotic rarity was, sadly, lost to the coco-de-mer when, towards the end of the 18th. century, the French took possession of the islands and laid bare the secrets of its origin. The island of Praslin – its secret uncovered – had to yield boatloads of the sought-after nuts. Not surprisingly, this arbitrary disregard of the laws of supply and demand led to the bottom dropping out of the market practically overnight. Disappointed tradesmen were left, so to speak, high and dry, as indeed – but in a slightly different manner – were the last remaining coco-de-mer palms: only about 4,000 of them remain now, in a relatively small area of rough terrain situated at the higher elevations in the heart of Praslin, and come under the protection of the Vallée de Mai National Park. Apart from a few isolated examples growing on the neighbouring island of Curieuse, this is and will remain – for a number of good reasons – the only habitat of the coco-de-mer in the whole world.

To start with, growth and propagation of the double-cheeked nut is a lengthy, drawn out affair. The germination period of the young sprout lasts a total of three years, and the process of maturing requires 7 years. The palm first bears fruit after about 25 years and doesn't reach its full height until it is about a 1,000 years old! It is estimated that the tallest palms in the Vallée de Mai, which reach to something like 130 ft., are about 800 years old.

Further, weight and volume of the fruit (at up to 40 lbs. the world's heaviest!) are distinct obstacles to the palms being able to extend their territory naturally. The complete fertile fruit sinks like lead, in water, and is therefore not able to be transported by the sea's currents. Even worse (for the palms): the salt water quickly makes the fruit infertile – irrevocably. This explains, however, why the coco-de-mer is able to reach such distant lands: once having "died" the fruit falls apart fairly rapidly, setting the nut itself, which is lighter, free to float away.

There is another impediment to propagation (applies also in case of manual transplantation): the female tree, which bears the precious fruit, needs to be in the vicinity of its male counterpart, the 2 inch thick and 3 ft. long olive brown "catkin" which bears an equally obvious resemblance to human anatomy as does the fruit of the female coco-de-mer. These similarities have not escaped the Seychellois attention and have proved to be the "stuff" of much speculation. There are those who will maintain that, on stormy nights, the sound of the huge leaves (which can reach a length of 18 ft. or more) slapping so noisily together, is that of the union of the male and female palms (mating cry, to the more imaginative); nobody of course, can claim to have been witness to such an event, not least of all because – as belief will have it – either ear or eyewitness shall come to a sticky end… The truth of the matter is a little more mundane: pollination, i.e. seed transfer from the orange-coloured blossoms of the male seed stock to the female palm, is effected by insects, the green geckos or just the wind.

The government allows 3,000 coco-de-mer nuts to be harvested annually. Some of them are consumed in the "green" state: the jelly-like contents of an approx. 9 month old nut are prized as a dessert. The rest are either crafted into fruit bowls and other vessels, or sold whole (polished brown or in the natural grey state) to tourists. This unique, but in no way cheap, souvenir was sold in 1983, at between £35 to £50 sterling. No two are exactly the same and it is said that there are as many differences to be found amongst them, as there are between their human, viz female counterparts. You will find the greatest available selection of nuts to choose from, at the government depot on Praslin. This is where all the nuts are stored.

Aldabra, Galapagos of the Indian Ocean

No competent scientist would take exception to mentioning the two island groups in the same breath, despite the differences which do exist between them. Both are places which play a decisively important role in natural history research, maintaing species which no longer exist elsewhere. There is not another enclave in this world where so many giant tortoises are able to live in total freedom.

You'll find Aldabra a good 700 miles south-west of the principal Seychelles island of Mahé, being thereby the most remote of the archipelago's constituent islands. It is another 400 odd miles to Africa and about 200 or so miles to Madagascar. Aldabra encompasses an area of 50 sq. miles; only about a dozen or so people live on it. One could easily fit the whole of Mahé and its 56,000 inhabitants into this, the largest lagoon and largest coral atoll in the world. It even lays claim to being the most remarkable island there is: 80,000 years ago there was a volcano, the tip of which is now – Aldabra. You could call it a giant mangrove-lined reservoir, with four gaps in it which function like the sluice gates of a lock, allowing the sea to pour in as the tide rises, and pour out again as it recedes – almost draining the lagoon completely and uncovering age-old, now lifeless mushroom-shaped banks of coral.

This is one of the marvels of Aldabra – the other is the unique assortment of animal life which has developed here. That this could even come about has a lot to do with the remote location of the island, and the rather unfriendly conditions it offered the settler, the first of whom incidentally, arrived here in 1899, planted coconuts which have given today's 2 miles long plantation on Grande Terre, and did what they could with what the sea had to offer in terms of fish and turtles. The rest of the atoll they left pretty much to itself, meaning business could proceed more or less as it had done for thousands upon thousands of years.

The giant tortoises here have, in the course of history, continually been hunted, and in 1842 two ships alone are reported to have taken no less than 1,200 of these animals. At the turn of the century their numbers had been so severely reduced, that an expedition to the island took three whole days to find even one tortoise. There were, however, obviously sufficient still around as, in 1982, 152,000 was the estimated count! The figure is asessed at around 180,000 today.

Still other animals have managed to find a good foothold on the island: more and more turtles are reported coming on land here (December to March) to lay their eggs, and between 6,000 and 7,000 white-breasted rails, which have lost the ability to fly, are also at home here. A further example of the indigenous bird life is the Aldabra ibis with its porcelain blue eyes. Sea birds, which flock to the atoll in their millions, include migratory birds such as flamingos and herons, numerous types of terns and the frigate bird of which Aldabra can boast the largest colony in the whole of the Indian Ocean.

The government has declared Aldabra a "protected zone" for wildlife, and no commercial activities are allowed. The only ones able to "reap reward" from this atoll, are the scientists who wish to do research work there, in this marvel of the Indian Ocean – and wildlife itself!

Hawksbill or loggerhead turtle (Eretmochelys imbricata)

Caretta turtle (Caretta caretta)

Historical Ups and Downs

Even the historians themselves don't agree about who first discovered the group of islands lying in the middle of the Indian Ocean, which we know as the Seychelles.

A fairly safe bet would tend to be the assumption that it was Arab traders, who, something like 1,000 years ago, whilst on their way across the Indian Ocean, were the first ones to drop anchor off the shallow waters of the Seychelles. Mention of a group of islands south of the Maldives, on charts dating back to the 9th century A.D., is the authority you could quote in substantiation of the assumption...

You're on safe ground if you then go on to mention that it was Vasco da Gama who, whilst circumnavigating the world during the 16th century, discovered the Amirante islands, which are nowadays counted as belonging to the Seychelles archipelago. Fact: in the year of our Lord 1609, Alexander Sharpeigh, the commander of a British East India Company expedition charged with finding new trading partners south of the Red Sea, was able to log that, after certain navigational difficulties, the ships "Ascension" and "Good Hope" were able, quite by chance, to find safe anchorage in the Seychelles. From ship's documents which were later made public, it is clear that these matelots were able to take ample stocks of coconuts, timber and fish, but that their incursions into these new territories yielded no visible evidence of their being inhabited. The conclusion would be that, up to that time at least, these islands in the middle of the Indian Ocean were indeed uninhabited!

Whether there is any connection or not is anybody's guess but, some short while later, the French, who had already taken over the neighbouring island of Mauritius (Isle de France), began increasingly often to put into the secluded bays on Mahé, Praslin and La Digue, for repair and/or to evade pirates. And one would probably not be too far off the mark to consider it as a tactical move on the part of Bertrand François Mahé de Labourdonnais, Governor General of the "Isle de France", to establish the islands as a supply base for the French fleet, in order to clearly define certain demarcation lines for the British fleet in the Indian Ocean.

Without there being too much red tape involved, he sent his man, a captain Picault, over to the islands, in 1742, and this marks the beginning of the official modern history of the Seychelles.

It was not until some 14 years later, in 1756, that the French captain Morphey was to install the "Stone of Possession" on the island of Mahé, hoist the flag of his King, Louis XV of France and, in honour of the King's chancellor, Moreau de Séchelles, give the islands the name under which we still know them today.

The Seychelles at a Glance

Form of Government: Republic with a single-chamber parliament and one political party, the Seychelles Peoples Progressive Front (SPPF) which elects the president and governing ministers. Since 1977, the offices of President, Chancellor and Minister for Trade have been combined in the person of Mr. France Albert Renée.

Territory: the total (land) surface area of the 100 or so Seychelles islands is 171 sq. miles; the total sovereign sea area of the Seychelles, located in the western sector of the Indian Ocean, totals about 155,000 sq. miles.

Population: named "Seychellois", including Negroes and mulattos, French Creoles and a minority of Indians, Chinese and Malays. Total: 64,000. Census according to island or island group: Mahé, 57,000; Praslin, 4,500; La Digue, 2,000; Silhouette, 250; other granite islands including Bird and Denis islands, 150; Amirantes, 250; Farquhar and Aldabra, 150.

Language of the people since 1981: Creole; the languages of officialdom are English and French. Apart from Creole, which is spoken by the majority of the population, English is the most common language.

Religions: 91% of the population are Catholics, 7,5% are professed Anglicans and the rest come under the heading of "various".

Most important Exports: copra, cinnamon, cinnamon oil, coconuts and guano. About 60% of foreign earnings are related to tourist activities. Main trading partners are: Great Britain, France and other members of the European Community, Pakistan, South Africa, Mauritius, Réunion, Kenya and the Peoples Republic of the Yemen.

In 1770 the first French settlers arrived, and with them also the first slaves. Following the French Revolution, in 1789, the English evidently thought that they might have a go at wresting control of the islands from the French. Insofar as one can be certain about exactly what took place so long ago, it seems that Quéau de Quinssy, installed as governor of the islands in 1794, was a bit of a joker: in the face of the enemy (the British in this case) he had the flag lowered, to signal his capitulation, and then – as soon as the victorious fleet (the British again) had sailed out of Mahé harbour – he had it hoisted again. The thing is, he tried this one no less than 7 times!

The last cat-and-mouse capitulation was played out in 1810, and British annexation of the islands was formally recognised by the Treaty of Paris (1814).

In recognition of de Quinssy's evident capability and popularity, the British powers that "were" offered to let him keep his job! He accepted and changed his name to de Quincy, which deference to British magnanimity is recorded for all to see, in the shape of a Mahé street named in his honour. For a period of 13 years, until 1827, he kept the lines of communication between the island's English and French inhabitants open. In fact, his political "savvy" was definitely a "lucky break" for the islands and largely set the political tone for some time to come.

In 1835 slavery was finally abolished, and this certainly had its effects on life in the islands: ex-slaves, many of whom had been pressed into service at sea, settled here. And just as Sinatra put it, in a song, "birds do it, let's fall in love," so did the people of the islands. This intermingling of the races has produced today's typically Seychellois breed of people.

The next historically significant date was 31st August, 1903: the islands gained the status of a British Crown Colony on this date. The political "doldrums" would describe well the situation the islands found themselves in for the ensuing half century. The isolation suffered by the islands because of the Great War did them no economic good at all. The depressions of the 20's and 30's did not help, nor did the 2nd World War, which, on top of it all, claimed a contingent of Seychelles soldiers.

Since 1964 the islands have been more or less politically autonomous; with British aid a system of parliamentary government was established and elections held. The 29th June, 1976, marked the official date for independence and the first President of the newly formed parliamentary Republic of the Seychelles was James R. Mancham who, under British rule, had previously held the post of Prime Minister. The current President of the Seychelles is M. France Albert Renée, who took office in 1977.

(Hedegaard)

History of the Seychelles, at a Glance

7th–10th century. Presumably first visited by Arab traders.

15th/16th century. First mention of the Seychelles islands on Portugese charts; Vasco da Gama discovers the Amirantes in 1502; Juan Nova discovers Farquhar island in 1504.

1609. A British East Indian Company expedition lands on the Seychelles.

17th/18th century. Pirates make use of the islands – as hide-outs and supply bases.

1742. The Frenchman, Lazare Picault, lands on the Seychelles in the name of Francois Mahé de la Bourdonnais, governor of the "Isle de France" (Mauritius), and gives the largest island the name "Ile d'Abondance".

1744. Lazare Picault is about again. On this journey he rechristens the "Ile d'Abondance", in honour of his governor, "Mahé".

1756. Captain Nicholas Morphey claims possession of the Seychelles in the name of his king, Louis XV, in honour of whose Chancellor of the Exchequer the islands receive the name "Séchelles".

1770. The first French settlers and numerous slaves land on the island of St. Anne.

1772. A second settlement is founded, at Anse Royale, on Mahé, to begin the cultivation of spices and vegetables.

1778. A third settlement, on Mahé, lays the foundation of what is to become the capital, Victoria.

1794. Quéau de Quinssy is appointed Governor of the Seychelles.

1794–1810. De Quinssy capitulates, in the face of the British, seven separate times.

1814. As provided for in the Treaty of Paris, the islands are ceded to the British Crown. The incumbent governor (under previous French rule) remains in office, under the British, until 1827.

1835. Slavery is abolished, by act of the British Parliament.

1851. The first Catholic diocese is founded in Victoria.

1893. The first lines of news communication to the outside world come into operation: a telegraph cable to Zanzibar and Mauritius.

1903. Administration of the Seychelles from Mauritius is ended. The island's status becomes that of a British Crown Colony.

1916/17. Volunteer corps take part in campaigns in Africa and India.

1923. Victoria is supplied with electricity.

1934. The Seychelles rupee becomes legal tender.

1948. A limited voting franchise is introduced.

1959. The first merchant bank is set up.

1964. Founding of the first political parties.

1970. The Seychelles achieve a degree of autonomy, under Prime Minister Mancham.

1971. The international airport comes into operation. Queen Elizabeth II attends the official opening ceremony the following year.

1976. The Seychelles become independant; James R. Mancham is the President, France Albert Reneé the Prime Minister.

1977. A coup d'état results in France Albert Reneé becoming President of the republic.

Location and Formation

You might recall having seen pictures of the Seychelles in a magazine or holiday brochure. And, I bet, something about the Seychelles will have caught your eye; something other than the usual palm trees, sun, sand and sea: you discover pink-tinged rock and cliff formations, some no bigger than you and others as big as "houses" and often with a remarkable sort of wavy finish to the surface, as though they had been specially ground or prepared – perhaps as props for a Hollywood film? Well, it's nothing of the sort. Nature it is, that has been at work here, and the Hollywood film architects are evidently not as practised as nature, in the art of "cliff finishing". And it is the very "special" effects indeed – achieved by the erosive forces of wind, water and sand, over millions of years – which draw not only the "moguls", but the pick of the world's photographers as well – all this way, just to embellish their beach scenes with the Seychelles' remarkable granite cliffs!

These typically cliff-backed beach scenes, looking like something straight out of a picture book, have become a sort of trade mark of the Seychelles, or at least to put it more precisely, of the so-called granite islands, which, rising up from that 7,800 sq. mile granite base, the Mahé plateau, constitute the popular tourist islands. They jut out of the ocean, like the tips of an underwater mountain range, reaching quite respectable heights: Mahé reaches about 2,980 ft. and the smaller islands of Praslin and La Digue claim 1,120 ft. and 1,110 ft. respectively. The mountains are relatively steep, as is particularly noticeable on Mahé. The bare rock can be seen shimmering through the dense vegetation over wider expanses of the mountain sides; the slopes are broken up by deep gullies and sheer cliff faces. There are no rivers in the normal sense, but hundreds of little streams can be seen cascading down the broken mountain terrain. Fertile land is a scarce commodity on the granite islands; there is usually a thin coastal belt of it, and even this is often broken up by small lakes or marsh land. The islands are lined with mangrove-covered shorelines and sandy beaches, but in many places granite cliffs or outcrops of rock extend down to the water or into the sea itself.

The granite which Mahé, Praslin, La Digue and some of the smaller islands are made up of, is amongst the oldest on earth. It dates back to the pre-cambrian era, and is thus some 650 million years old! The syenite and micro-syenite of Silhouette and North Island date back too, but not quite so far: the tertiary period, presumably. The seabed around the islands is made up of layers of fossilised coral, which, in places, has formed protective reefs. The formation of coral islands seems to have been restricted to the northern edge of the Mahé Plateau, and Bird and Denis islands are the most convenient examples of this "other" type of island to visit – if you're coming from Mahé, that is. Not far from these islands the shallow waters of the Mahé Plateau (depth between 100 ft. and 200 ft.) give way to the enormous deep of the Indian Ocean proper: the seabed drops steeply down to a depth of some 6,000 ft. and more. You can see why the islands are a good base for the deep-sea fisher.

All the remaining islands, lying outside the perimeter of the Seychelles Plateau, are coral atolls. There are some 50 of these, whereas there are only 40 granite islands. It is difficult to come up with the exact number of islands, because sometimes the count will include even tiny little islands – some would better be described as sandbanks, some as mere granite rocks – and other times these will be overlooked. However, whether or not this or that little outcrop is included in the Seychelles' territorial inventory, is really unimportant and wouldn't change anything about this remarkably far-flung island domain called the Seychelles archipelago. For instance: whilst the coral atolls of the Amirantes group are less than 200 miles from Mahé, you'll find the Farquhar group is more like 500 miles distant, and the Aldabra group close on 700 miles away. For that though, the distance from Aldabra to the Kenyan coastline, in Africa, is only about 400 miles, and from Farquhar to the northern tip of Madagascar you would notch up say, 250 miles.

That the Seychelles might, at some time, have been connected to the nearest larger landmass, i.e. Madagascar, is, according to geologists, a false assumption. Firstly the granite of the Mahé Plateau is part of the Mascarene Ridge, which, along the sea-bed of the Indian Ocean, describes an arc over a distance of about 1,600 miles and extends to the islands of Mauritius and Réunion, and not towards Madagascar. Secondly, scientists tend towards the belief that the Seychelles were, at one time, part of a sub-continent which connected Africa with India, or that they are the fragmented remains of the continental displacement of Africa and India.

Be that as it may, for certain is the fact that the millions of years of isolation in which the islands have existed, have allowed the primeval terrain and life-forms to remain in existence in a way in which it has not been possible elsewhere. Scientists would not hesitate to compare the Seychelles, in terms of evolutionary significance, to the Galapagos islands. More of this under another heading.

Climate, and when to go

A long flight and then, in accordance with local regulations, a mandatory flight-cabin disinfection behind you, you are finally able to disembark; you take in a deep breath of long-awaited fresh air. Seychelles air. And then you either get a shock or are enchanted. Shocked, perhaps, by the seeming humidity which envelopes you; enchanted, most definitely, by the delightful tropical warmth which greets you, as if to signal that you've arrived – on holiday at last!

Both reactions are absolutely normal, because people's reactions to changes in climate are as varied as people themselves. And then, your body quite naturally needs some time to adjust from the cool, drier air-conditioned cabin environment, to the warm, moisture-laden tropical air. Within two to three days you should have all that behind you. One factor which influences the time your body needs to adapt to the new conditions is the time-lag involved (you're in a different timezone). Fortunately the time difference (for the European, at least) is not too great: the islands are at G.M.T. – 3 hours, whereas on the Carribbean or south-east Asian holiday isles, your "biological clock" can be as much as 6 or 8 hours off beam.

The main holiday islands of the Seychelles, i.e. the so-called Mahé group, being situated just 4°C south of the equator, are blessed with basically pretty constant climatic conditions the whole year round. Statistics show a mean annual temperature of 26.7°C (80°F) from which value average monthly highs only deviate marginally, range within the 26.2°C (79°F) in July, to 27.7°C (82°F) in May. Relative atmospheric humidity stays at about 80% throughout the year: a moderate reading for tropical climes. The effect of cooling breezes which blow in from across the sea the whole year round – apart from in the monsoon "turnaround" periods of April/May and October/November – is to provide a pleasant, tropical sea climate.

The influence of the monsoons determines the fact that the Seychelles experience two predominant and distinctly different seasonal periods annually:

* a cooler, drier season, when the south-east trade winds blow, from May to October;
* a hotter, wetter season, during which the north-west monsoon blows, from December until well into March.

Between the seasons is the monsoon "turnaround" period, during which you get times of almost complete calm, i. e. no wind at all; because of the accompanying heat, some people find these periods uncomfortably hot and close, whilst others revel in it. "You pays yer money, and you takes yer pick", as they say.

When the north-west monsoon comes, it rains. Better perhaps: it rains more often, because you get rain here all year round. It's just that in the monsoon season it rains more frequently, more intensely, more suddenly – but generally not for long, one must add. You could even be lucky enough to find that these sudden downpours only occur at nighttime, and so, should you be sleeping, they needen't bother you at all. But even so, should you be caught, during the daytime, in a squall, look at it this way: to start with the rain is warm; there will definitely not be any cold wind blowing, so – one presumes you've got the right sort of light, cotton clothes on – you'll find that the agreeable tropical warmth will have dried you out again completely, in little more than the time it took to drench you.

When the north-west monsoon blows here it is winter time in Europe, and this is the reason for it being the main tourist season on the islands. A further reason for it being a good time to come here is that, with the first few good rain showers, everything starts to positively "burst" with life; the blossoming flowers and lush, spreading vegetation give both man and beast that "lift", that feeling of being "glad to be alive". The keen photographer will find the imposing cloud formations, so typical for this time of year, good subjects to "snap". On the other hand, holidaymakers whose hotels are situated on the west coast of Mahé, those at Beau Vallon Bay principally, may not be quite so enamoured of the gusty winds and high seas; at times the waves breaking vehemently onto the beach are better admired from a distance.

Climatic Table Mahé/Victoria (Airport)

Month	Daily high °C °F	Nightly low °C °F	Daily hours of sunshine	Humidity mid- in %	No. of days with rain	Rainfall in mm
January	29 84	24 75	6	83	22	380
February	29 84	25 77	6	77	15	230
March	30 86	25 77	7	78	16	250
April	30 86	25 77	8	80	15	180
May	31 88	25 77	8	79	14	200
June	28 82	25 77	7	79	14	100
July	27 81	24 75	7	81	12	100
August	27 81	24 75	7	81	11	150
September	28 82	24 75	7	81	12	150
October	28 82	24 75	7	83	13	250
November	29 84	24 75	7	83	17	350
December	29 84	24 75	6	82	20	350

Conversely, when the south-east trade winds blow, the hotels on the east coast get the "best" of the "blow". They blow more strongly and are more constant – especially during the months of June to August – than their north-west counterpart, and are a boon to windsurfers, i.e. those who know what they're about. The whole of the east coast is also much, much drier than the rest of Mahé. The reason being that the mountains, which attract the clouds and on the slopes of which they increasingly (as they gain altitude) turn into rain, are some distance away.

The mountainous islands have (therefore) much more rainfall annually than do the flatter islands. Silhoutte, and the higher elevations of Mahé can get as much as 3,000 mm (120 inches). Praslin and La Digue record between 1,500 mm (60 inches) and 2,000 mm (80 inches) annually – and a good portion of all this precipitation will have come down between the months of November and January. The much flatter coral islands, e. g. Bird or Denis island, will usually only get a fraction of the amount of rain which falls on say, Mahé.

A few more facts on the subject of climate: the Seychelles lie outside the cyclone belt, so that bad thunderstorms are rare occurrences; the sun rises at pretty much the same time throughout the year, at about 6.30 am, setting, similarly, after only a short period of twilight, at around 6.30 pm; the temperature of the sea, at between 26 to 30°C is pleasant to bathe in all year round.

The best time to come? For those who would prefer the cooler, drier, more windy season: between May and October (July and August are pretty busy months). For those who prefer it a bit warmer, wouldn't mind the odd rain shower and aren't put off by the humidity being a few points higher: December to March (greatest influx of tourists in the period mid-December to mid-January). If you prefer a more relaxed, quiet holiday and can arrange to come in April or May or in October/November you'll find nigh on empty hotels, no wind – to speak of –, calm seas and higher temperatures, and (bad for some) the occasional period of close weather to greet you.

The local Flora and Fauna

Islands, especially those which, like the Seychelles, enjoy such a "splendidly" isolated location, have always been a particular source of attraction to both the professional and hobby botanist and zoologist. Over millions of years, many sorts of plants and animals have been able to develop and adapt along specific lines and into characteristically specialised species, allowing extremely informative comparisons to be made between them and their original "relatives" in their country or continent of origin. As most (land) animals and plants either cannot, or would find it extremely difficult to cross the ocean, their presence on a particular island would indicate that, in the past, there must have been a connection of some sort or another to a neighbouring landmass. Conversely, their absence would indicate the opposite.

Mammals are an interesting case in point: they play second fiddle – or are conspicuous by their absence in the fauna of the so-called "oceanic islands" (such as are not close to any continental landmass) like the Seychelles, because of the watery divide. Apart from the mammals brought over to the islands by man (the rat and the mouse, the cat and dog, goat and horse) the islands have precious little to offer. The one mammal they do have is a bat; the fruit bat, commonly called the "flying fox" (Pteropus seychellensis) This large member of the bat family has a head rather like a dog's; it feeds principally on fruit, only flies out at night and is then usually mistaken for a bird. If you'd like to see the fruit bat yourself then take a trip to the botanical gardens of the Boutique Macouti at Beau Vallon, Mahé. Be warned, however, that conditions for the animals there are not ideal.

What's true for the mammals is also largely true for the **reptiles** – insofar as they don't just happen to be expert swimmers, as is the turtle

(even the tortoise has a pronounced natural ability to swim). Smaller reptiles will possibly have made good use of pieces of floating wood or other such flotsam, or smuggled themselves aboard a boat, in order to put greater nautical miles behind themselves. And so, you do find the smaller reptile, in the shape of the skink, the gecko, the chameleon and the smaller types of snake at home in, or having at sometime or another "stowed away" to, the Seychelles, but no big snakes. "That's a relief", did you say? The three – harmless – types of adder you get here do their utmost to stay out of harm's way but the agile little gecko can often be seen scampering about in the trees. With the exception of those on Mahé – evidently having learnt something to their personal advantage – the house gecko loves to climb about on the outsides of houses and bungalows (the dwellings) in search of insects, contributing, in his own small way, to your being able to enjoy an untroubled night's sleep. The green gecko, on the other hand, is rather more cautious and stays mainly in the trees or bushes. You'll often find him in banana trees; he also plays a most useful role for the coco-de-mer palms: that of pollinator.

Once upon a time the granite islands of the Seychelles were home to some larger sorts of reptiles, principally the cayman, the crocodile and the tortoise. All, save for the tortoise, have been mercilessly hunted down and wiped out by man. That the tortoise should survive is almost a miracle as, even in times before the islands were first settled, ships passing the islands would take quantities of them as "live" rations. They would be left lying, still alive, upside down on their shells, until at some stage they would be slaughtered and eaten. The original settlers, one might add, were in the habit of doing the same; tortoise meat, as opposed to fish, provided a desirable alternative source of protein. As tortoises don't multiply very quickly (they are first capable of reproducing at an age of about 20 years), they were very soon also near to extinction. Today there are only very few left, including some magnificent examples such as Esmeralda and

Agamemnon on Bird Island. Esmeralda – a misnoma incidentally, because it turned out to be a male specimen – counts as the oldest, largest and heaviest tortoise on earth: over 150 years old with, as scientifically established in 1981, a shell measuring all of 63 inches.

A number of small communities of tortoises are on view in enclosures on the island of Cousin (including the senior beast, named "Georges", presumably over 100 years old) and in the Victoria Botanical Garden on Mahé. The odd pair are also privately kept, e. g. by hotels. They all come from the island of Aldabra, which, apart from the Galapagos Islands, is the last remaining natural refuge where these tortoises are still able to roam free. At the turn of the century the Aldabra population had declined to only a few thousand, but decisive and rigorous measures were taken to preserve and protect these animals so that the community had increased to 152,000 by the year 1982, and has been estimated at 182,000 at the end of 1983. (See also: "Aldabra, Galapagos of the Indian Ocean")

The island's turtles would actually come under the heading of reptiles as well, but you can read more about them in the chapter: "Fascinating Underwater World."

Birds, insects and certain seeds and plants which may easily be carried by the wind have few obstacles placed in the way of their getting to a remote oceanic island. The fact that out of the 21 species of land birds which are indigenous to the Seychelles, 13 should also be exclusive to these islands, lends support to the supposition that the islands must have existed in isolation from other continental land masses for a very, very long time. Interesting to note is that all the species, despite being exlusive to these islands, do have "distant relations" in other regions and are evidently not quite as unique as the – now alas extinct – Mauritius dodo. All the same, the wealth of land birds to be found on the Seychelles can doubtless provide both professional and hobby ornithologists with some fascinating hours.

As the distribution of most of the species is restricted to two or three islands (principally outside of Mahé), you will need to devote quite some (enjoyable) time to the task of tracking them down. A measure of success is certainly to be achieved over a period of say, 14 days, during which you will have had a chance to pay a visit to "Bird Island", home of an extraordinary wealth of sea birds, as well.

Detailed information as to markings, habitat and habits of the various birds can be gleaned from the pages of the literature we recommend in the index. Here a list of the endemic (exlusive to the Seychelles) species and subspecies which you have a good chance of "spotting" during your travels, and hints on where to find them.

Black Parrot (Coracopsis nigra barklyi) – Vallée de Mai National

Park on Praslin, on and around all types of fruit trees.

Magpie Robin (Copsychus seychellarum) – on the Frégate Plateau, on the ground; rather than spend too much time on the drinks included in the day return air "Hop" fare, you should get on your way as soon as you can – the higher the sun climbs, the fewer birds you'll find.

Black Paradise Flycatcher (Tchitrea corvina), also known by the locals as the "veuve" (the widow) – found on La Digue, where the René Payet Veuve Réserve has been established.

Brush Warbler (Bebrornis seychellensis) – on Cousin, in the Cousin Island Nature Reserve.

Seychelles Turtle Dove (streptopelia picturata rostrata) – on Cousin Island.

Seychelles Blue Pigeon (Alectroenas pulcherrima) – on the Mahé heights, the Frégate Plateau and in the Vallée de Mai on Praslin.

Seychelles Sunbird (Nectarinia dussumieri) – on all types of blossoming shrubs and on nearly all the larger islands.

Seychelles Kestrel (Falco araea) – on Mahé, on buildings and telegraph poles etc.

Seychelles Fody (Foudia seychellarum), also known by the locals as the "toc toc" – on Cousin, Cousine and Frégate.

Seychelles Grey White-Eye (Zosterops modesta) – on the Mahé highlands.

Seychelles Bulbul (Hypsipetes crassirostris) – in the highland forests of all the granite islands.

Three of the species which have made their home in the Seychelles will attract your attention particularly: the **cattle egret,** which favours coconut groves as much as the fish market (not excluding Victoria's), evidently feels equally comfortable around rubbish-dumps and could, in a way, be viewed as a substitute for the lack of seagulls in the Seychelles; the delicate, **barred ground dove** (Geopelia striata), which will come perkily hopping around you if you happen to be eating out in the open; and the bright red-feathered **Madagascar fody** (Foudia madagascariensis), also called serin, or cardinal, in Creole, which is both the most common and the most colourful bird on all the islands.

The Seychelles function as, you could say "bases" for **the seabirds of the Indian Ocean,** and thus count amongst the bird's most important biospheres. The shallow waters of the Mahé Plateau are a plentiful source of food and the (almost) uninhabited islands, such as Bird Island, Aride and Cousin harbour neither man nor beast as predator. Strict regulations for the protection of wildlife are also in force and international institutions, such as the Royal Society, support these measures. The regulations apply especially to those islands outside of the Mahé Plateau, which are favoured by seabirds, e.g. African Banks and Desnoeufs (Amirantes group), Goëlette (Farquhar group) as well as Aldabra and Cosmoledo (Aldabra group). Because these islands are so out-of-the-way, the seabird communities have, to all intents and purposes, been able to exist here undisturbed. In the normal course of a holiday, a visit to these islands will prove difficult because they are not serviced regularly by air and accomodation is a problem, too. This is in part, perhaps, a conscious concession to the interests of preservation. Special interest groups, such as ornithologists or divers, will find it worthwhile chartering a schooner from either Victoria or La Digue (see also "Useful Information").

By comparison, the first group of above mentioned bird islands – Bird Island itself, Aride and Cousin – are easily accessible. For instance, there is a daily flight from Mahé to Bird Island (flight duration approx. 40 minutes). Travel agencies in Victoria offer day trips there, but often one will find oneself so enchanted by the island and the bird life it supports, that one is left wishing that one had booked a tour lasting several days, which, alas, can only be booked in advance. So, one should think about booking this trip, back home, when initially arranging one's holiday – or see what can be fixed up with one of the agencies in Victoria. You get to the other two bird islands by boat: Aride – Mahé is 1½ hours, and Praslin – Aride takes half an hour. Disembarking – if that's the right word – can be a bit of a problem (even impossible) if the sea is rough or the wind too strong, because of the off-shore reefs; Cousin welcomes groups of maximum 20 people each, on Tuesdays, Fridays and Saturdays only. Information on currently available tours is available from your hotel or local travel agents.

Of the indigenous Seychelles seabirds – and this includes all but one species – the **terns** are the most numerous and also provide the exception: the **sooty tern** (Sterna fuscata). These birds literally swarm in their millions to their traditional nesting places, principally on Bird Island but also on the African Banks (Amirante Islands), during April/May and October/November; Aride and Cousin also experience a definite influx of these, our feathered friends, during these months too. It might sound a bit like a fairy-tale, but it's true: exactly where they have come from or where they go to, in the intervening months, is a mystery to ornithologists. It is concievable – even, that they stay "aloft" over a period of several months. Well, that's what some say.

Here now some brief details about the most important of the indigenous Seychelles seabirds.

Fairy Tern (Gygis alba monte) – perhaps the most charming of the terns, white with a blue beak and

1. White-Tailed Tropic Bird
2. Great Frigate
3. Black Paradise Flycatcher
4. Fairy Tern
5. Sooty Tern

black eyes; it lays its single egg not in a nest, but simply in the fork of a tree or just on the ground. To be found on almost all the islands, they increasingly fell victim, especially on Mahé, to the Africa Barn Owl (Tyto alba affinis) which had been imported during the early fifties by the planters to keep the rats down. Since the owl has been declared fair game for hunters, the number of fairy terns has visibly increased.

Roseate Tern (Sterna dougalii arideensis) – the most colourful of the terns with its red feet and red and black beak; Aride has the world's largest colony and smaller ones exist on Bird Island, for example.

Common Noddy (Anous Stolidus, also called Maqua) – found on all the islands, but mostly on Bird Island; brown coloured; breeds principally in coconut palms.

Lesser Noddy (Anous tenuirostris, also called cordonnier, the "cobbler") – exclusively an inhabitant of Cousin, Cousine and Aride islands; largest colony found on Aride.

Greater Frigate and **Lesser Frigate** (Fregata ariel, Fregata minor) – possibly the most acrobatic of fliers (around these parts). Because of their wing span of up to 6 ft., they have (extreme) difficulty landing (thus they, infact, don't) on the water, and so they use their considerable skills to relieve other birds, such as the terns or boobys, of their booty, in flight; whereas larger colonies of them are found to nest only on Aldabra, the birds can be spotted over all the granite islands, especially Aride and Fregate.

White-Tailed Tropic Bird (Phaeton lepturus) – on Bird Island, Cousin and Aride, but also on the Mahé heights.

Red-Tailed Tropic Bird (Phaethon aethereus) – is the rarest of all the Seychelles seabirds and takes to the air mainly over Aldabra and Cosmoledo but can also be seen on Aride.

Wedge-Tailed Shearwater (Puffinus pacificus) – on Cousin and Aride; breeds November/March; dark grey colour with pink feet.

Audubon's Shearwater (Puffinus l'herminieri) – a bit smaller than the Wedge-Tailed Shearwater and is white-breasted; Cousin has some, Aride more.

Two of the sorts of birds which you only see on the islands distant from Mahé are worth mentioning too: the **Red-Footed Booby** (Sula sula rubripes) seems to like it on Farquhar, Cosmoledo and Aldabra just as much as the **Blue-Faced** or **Masked Booby** (Sula dacylatra melanops) does on Cosmoledo, which is his "patch".

A great variety of migratory birds can periodically be spotted on the Seychelles islands, including: curlew sandpiper, grey plover, whimbrel, turnstone and sanderling and, on Aldabra, **flamingos** and **herons.**

The Seychelles **flora,** this abundant lush tropical vegetation, is undeniably a sight to gladden the heart of any and every visitor to these shores. The palms with their long (waving) or fan-shaped fronds, the variety of colour in the blossoms of the shrubs, overhanging trees with dark-green leaves looking as though they'd been specially polished up for inspection, or trees with strange-looking fruit hanging on them – all this (and more) makes for an exotic, even enchanting atmosphere. And that's fair comment about the realm of plants in tropical latitudes.

Nonetheless, what you're seeing is an, as it were, "2nd generation" of flora. The 1st generation which had evolved over many hundreds of millions of years, was almost completely destroyed by man in a little under 200 years. Once, a tropical forest of giant trees must have covered the islands – the granite islands especially – with a dense roof of leaves reaching from the coastline, well up into the mountain heights. Despite having expressed their amazement and wonder at the sight of them, and rather than spare a thought for posterity and at least put down a detailed description of them, the first arrivals on these shores found no more pressing task than relentlessly to denude the terrain.

You may well have guessed it: yes, there are, luckily, one or two enclaves where the vegetation at least approximates the above description: in the less accessible, higher elevations on Mahé, on Silhouette Island and in the Vallée de Mai on Praslin which boasts a renowned, classic example of the Seychelles' palm forests.

Some, certainly, of the endemic forms of plant life typical of the Seychelles islands have prevailed, but they are now of only secondary importance in comparison with the great number of imported species which have, in the meantime, become established and represent the abovementioned "2nd" generation of flora.

Still, there are no less than 81 endemic species of plants on the Seychelles (i.e. such as do not appear anywhere else). Should your appetite have been whetted, then refer to the index, and the reference to the literature will point you in the direction of some interesting little publications, including ones covering plant life – the only trouble is, you'll have to go to the Seychelles to pick them up. Some of the more noteworthy examples of the endemic flora which you will doubtless come to notice whilst you're on the Seychelles are:

First off, the much-lauded **coco-de-mer** (Lodoicea maldivica/Lodoicea seychellarum), the double-cheeked coconut which now, as already mentioned, only grows in the Vallée de Mai on Praslin. (See also the chapters: "Highlights" and "Coco-de-Mer, the Fruit that came out of the sea".)

Five other varieties of endemic palms which are also worth mentioning are the **palmiste palm** (Deckenia nobilis) as well as four **latanier palms** (Nephrosperma vanhoutteeana, Roscheria melanochaetes, Phoenicophorium borsigianum and Verschaffeltia splendida). These can be seen in the Vallée de Mai too, as well as in the botanical gardens at Victoria.

An example of an endemic plant which is to be found growing in the higher elevations of Mahé and Silhouette (on the latter island particularly on Mont Pot à-Eau) is the **pitcher plant** (Nepenthes pervillei), the "pitchers" of which serve as insect traps. Interesting to see is how both the endemic vegetation which has spread naturally, and the purpose-planted, imported vegetation, introduced by man, have established themselves side by side in the various vegetation zones. A few titbits of information on the subject should satisfy the specialist, and those whose interest has been aroused.

The first vegetation zone is represented by the flora of the **coastal areas** and **lowlands** (lowland rainforests) up to elevations of about 1,000 ft. In these areas, naturally, the effects of man's influence are most noticeable, partly out of convenience and partly because of the proximity to, and incidence of cultivated and purpose-planted vegetation. Most commonly found here are: **coconut palms** (Cocos nucifera, often growing free); **mangroves** (Rhizophora mucronata, Avicennia marina); **takamaka** (Calophyllum inophylum); **vare** (Hibiscus tiliaceus); **bois blanc** (Hernandia ovigera); **badamier** (Terminalia catappa); **casuarien** (Casuarina equisetifolia); **bois rouge** (Noewormia ferruginea); **bois de natte** (Imbricaria seychellarum); **capucin** (Northea seychellarum); **bois de table** (Heritiera littoralis); **gayac** (Intsia bijuga); **banyan** (Ficus benghalensis).

Quick-growing or foreign species were employed for reafforestation purposes: **albizzia** (Albizzia falcataria); **agati** (Ademanthera pavonina); **flamboyant** (Delonix regia); **eucalyptus** (Eucalyptus sp.); **santol** (Sandoricum indicum); **sang dragon** (Precarcus indicus).

The **intermediate vegetation zone** (elevations from 1,000 to 2,000 ft.) exhibits an abundance of species: many of those of the first zone plus orchids, bamboo, cinnamon etc., as well as trees such as capucin, bois rouge and bois de montagne.

Elevations of 2,000 ft. and higher provide the **upper vegetation zone,** showing typical cloud forest conditions and having an annual rainfall of in excess of 80″. The most common types of trees are **capucin, bois rouge, latanier hauban** (Roscheria melanochaetes) and **cassant** (Timonius seychellensis).

Even if these names don't mean much to you, the pleasure you derive from the sight of the Seychelles' lush and blossoming flora will be a constant companion to you during your stay on the islands – irrespective of the time of year.

To witness the virtual "explosion" of blossom and flower all over the islands, brought on by the first heavy rains, you should time your visit for November/December. Above all, the widely sweeping, brilliant red flowering stock of the ornamental tree, "Flamboyant" will enthrall you, time and again.

A last tip: even if you're no more than mildly interested in things botanical, you shouldn't miss visiting the botanical gardens at Victoria. Here, apart from getting a good insight into the Seychelles' flora, you can see a few smaller specimens of coco-de-mer, giant tortoises in their enclosure and an orchid garden showing about 150 different species.

Fascinating Underwater World

The warm and pleasant waters of the Seychelles are home to an incredible and colourful variety of tropical marine life. The coral reefs, so fascinating in themselves, provide the ocean fauna with an ideal and safe retreat – sanctuary one might even say – and something like 300 different species of fish are known to inhabit these reefs. The government's determined conservation policy will, on the other hand, also have played a decisive role in allowing fish stocks to flourish; several marine nature reserves have been established, the best known of which will doubtless be the "Ste. Anne Marine National Park" lying directly off Victoria, thus allowing you easy access to the wonders of the underwater world. Harpooning is strictly prohibited, and in certain designated areas, "shelling" – i.e. the taking of shells, mussels etc. – either underwater or on the beach, is also prohibited.

All this has led to the fact that the Seychelles coral banks – and the teeming life they support – present a picture which contrasts most agreeably with that of many reefs in other parts of the world, which have been so arbitrarily plundered and virtually "cleared out". The fish here don't take man for a dangerous intruder, and are moreover so tame that they will literally eat out of your hand.

Although, this particularly impressive and pleasureable experience will necessarily be reserved for those divers who are able to stay down long enough to "make friends", as it were, with the "little chaps" down there, it's a lot of fun just diving down under the surface of the water with only a snorkel mask on, and finding the fish "carrying on regardless" – as though you didn't exist. And so you can, at your leisure, move about underwater, and observe our sub-aquatic friends "doing their thing" in and amongst the brain, elkhorn and other types of coral.

Of the approximately 2,500 types of coral there are, over a 100 are indigenous to the waters of the Seychelles – red, blue, white and black coral. The fantastic colouring and markings of the various fish stand out against this backdrop so well: for instance, that shining, brilliant flash of colour varying from anywhere between orange to cobalt blue, signifying the parrot fish which likes to nibble away at the coral with its hard, horny beak, or the browny-red lion fish (beware of the poisonous spiny fins) and the yellow, black and white butterfly fish with its long, pointed mouth, ideally siuted to "winkling" out its prey from nooks and crannies in the coral beds.

You know, even if the names (some as exotic as the fish themselves) of the various fish such as e.g. clown fish, emperor fish, zebra fish, angel fish, mother of pearl fish or trumpet fish don't mean a sausage to you, it doesn't detract in the least from the genuine pleasure to be had from seeing all these little fellows at first hand in their natural, unspoilt environment; tips on how you can best capture some of these great underwater scenes on celluloid, are given in the chapter "Photo Tips".

The reefs though, are only one of many areas (biospheres) which will come to mean unforgettable memories of the Seychelles for you. And

two of them lie beyond the reefs. One is that relatively shallow expanse of sea which covers the great underwater plateau from which the granite islands of the Mahé and Praslin group rise up. In these crystal clear waters in which underwater visibility is good up to about 50 yds., live the somewhat larger species of fish, such as bat fish, powder-blue surgeon fish, harlequin sweetlips and spotted moray eels. (Cast an eye over the chapter: "Underwater Sports on the Seychelles", and you'll get a scuba and snorkel diver's impression of these waters.)

The other, third area is represented by the "border line" between the shallow waters of the plateau and the 6,000 ft. deep of the Indian Ocean. Here, not far from the coral islands of Bird and Denis, where the plateau comes to an abrupt end and the seabed drops almost vertically down into the deep, tuna and sharks, barracudas and wahoos, sailfish and marlins romp in the open sea – providing the deep-sea angler with good sport, and plenty of it.

At home in all three of the above-mentioned biospheres you also find mussels and snails. The Seychelles have about 100 different species, the most common are the cowry snails and the conus snails. The former stand out because of their porcelain-like, light or dark coloured and variously striped shiny upper surface. Certain species of the latter have harpoon-like spines which one should be extremely wary of (poisonous). The Terebrides and Charonia tritonis snails are examples of nature's little works of art, and are a source of delight: the great triton is one of these.

And still there's more to see in this underwater paradise of the Seychelles; more than coral, fish and mussels. Meant is the turtle. Three species exist here: the hawksbill turtle (Eretmochelys imbricata), the mock turtle (Caretta caretta) and the green turtle (Chelonia mydas). The first two types you'll find in the waters of most of the islands throughout the year, whereas the latter stick pretty much to the Aldabra and Cosmoledo areas and hardly ever show their faces around the granite islands.

Unfortunately for the green turtle, it makes for an extremely tasty dish and has, over the years, graced many a cooking pot; one presumes that that is why it steers well-clear of the more populated islands. It now enjoys the specific protection of the government; provision has been made to set a limit on the number which may annually be trapped in the Seychelles waters. This figure will vary between 300 and 500. Worth noting is the fact that the western portion of Indian Ocean is the only region on earth where the green turtle is not (yet) counted an "endangered species". The number of turtles, which, according to the government quota, may be taken, palls into insignificance when seen in comparison with the numbers of eggs and baby turtles which fall prey each year to predators such as seabirds, crabs and fish. One somewhat remarkable fact about the green turtle is this: amongst those who would snatch (green turtle) eggs, you have to count the male green turtle himself! Small wonder then, that the annual catch quota refers explicitly to him.

Not only to be found over a larger area but also numerically superior, are the other two types of turtle, the hawksbill turtle and the carette turtle.

The hawksbill himself is prized because he (poor fellow) can be turned into the best (commercial) tortoiseshell. And tortoiseshell is of no mean importance to the economy of the Seychelles, insofar as it is a commodity sought-after by the textile industry. Thus tortoiseshell means jobs, and money for many people on Mahé and Praslin. And of course, it's also fashioned into jewellry, mainly directed at the tourist industry.

Even though the hawksbill turtle is alive, well and plentiful in the pleasant waters of the Seychelles, its situation worldwide (e. g. in the Caribbean) is not such a happy one, and it is therefore on the list of species covered by the Washington "**C**onvention on **I**nternational **T**rade in **E**ndangered **S**pecies of Wild Fauna and Flora in Commerce **(CITES).** Those countries which subscribe to this convention prohibit the importation of turtle shells and items made of tortoiseshell (see also "Souvenirs… Souvenirs…")

The commercial Aspect

The simple fact that you're going to be spending your holiday in a sunshine Garden of Eden like the Seychelles, presupposes that you have, or will want to forget the "hassles" of life – at least for a while. But they exist here too; for instance problems of a commercial nature.

Apart from nature having blessed them with a rich and exotic variety of fauna and flora, apart from being able to call an enviable climate and a surfeit of sun and warmth their own, and apart from the stunning beauty of the countryside and beaches, the Seychelles have precious few commercially exploitable (at least none as yet identified) natural resources, either above or below ground level. Even the ground itself can be seen as only a "reluctant" asset: only about 50% is suitable for cultivation, this figure including the coastal strips which are covered in coconut palms. Only about 10% of the surface area of Mahé can be used for agricultural purposes e. g. for the cultivation of vegetables, the remaining 90% consists of mountains, forest, beaches and cliffs.

And this has given rise to one of the Seychelles' major current problems: the maintenance of adequate supplies to cover the needs of the indigenous population and the periodic influx of tourists. In earlier, "pretourist" days the sea provided sufficient fish and the plantations enough copra, spices, fruit and vegetables etc. for a correspondingly smaller population. Nowadays things aren't what they used to be! Although production has, in fact, been successfully maximised in all but the fishery sector, the task of providing a population and holidaymaker count (seasonally varied), both of which have increased in comparable proportion, does remain a burden.

And so, the only thing left to do, is to import foodstuffs: meat from Australia, butter from Singapore or Holland, cheese from France whence, as well as from South Africa, wine for the tourist, to say nothing of luxury items such as expensive spirits and cigarettes.

It's the old vicious circle: without the imports, no tourists, and without the tourists, no imports, none even for domestic consumption. Statistics reveal the economic significance of imports: of the amount of currency which flows into the Seychelles' coffers from tourism – and this makes up about 60% of all foreign income – more than two thirds goes towards satisfying the needs of those self-same tourists! Unfortunately, domestic produce only represents a small proportion of total consumption, a much smaller proportion than in say, Kenya, another tourist oriented country. Additionally, the Seychelles have a development project in hand for the east coast of Mahé, including the improvement of the road network between Victoria and the airport. A rather ambitious project is proposed which will lead the highway between the coastline and the reef – in the same way as the international airport (finished in 1971) was built. Because the coastal strip is so thin, there was no place (other than into the sea) for it to be built. The cement required for the present project has all to be imported, because the pink granite, which is the only sort the islands have to offer, is unsuitable. You see, imports again, ton after ton.

All this serves to identify the sort of problems that the country faces, a country which has struggled for political independence and also seeks to achieve economic independence. And don't forget, there are only 64,000 people living in this country.

One little trick of fate's, which won't have escaped you, is that time doesn't stand still and neither do the now ever increasing demands made of life by the Seychellois. The islands' traditional export products, copra and spices, still have their markets open to them, but pressure of world competition makes itself felt in that sales trends are not neces-

There's Copra, and there's Copra

First of all, what is copra? Copra is the coconut kernel in the dried, and shredded state. Further, it consists of 60–65% fat, about 20% carbohydrate, about 8% protein and about 4% water; when pressed, it yields coconut oil which is used for the production of glycerine and is the basic constituent of synthetic resins; the refined coconut fat is turned into edible fats and also used in the manufacture of candles, soap and shampoo.

This mini-definition is good for copra, but says nothing about the actual quality of the product itself. And that's where the Seychellois have a trump up their sleeves: their copra is amongst the best in the world – a fact which is confirmed by trade specialists, scientists, chemists and consumers all over the globe. The main customers are the Pakistanis: they buy up practically the whole of the annual crop and are thereby the country's number one export customer. In 1981 they bought 17 million rupees worth; Réunion, the number two customer spent a little over 4 million in the same period.

The Pakistanis import their copra not in the "shredded" state, but as "copra cup" i. e. as halved nuts, including the hard, fibrous shell. There are reasons of both a culinary and religious nature for this. In Pakistan, which is an Islamic state, certain religious ceremonies require that the faithfull eat out of a communal pot. They scoop up the rice and spices from the communal pot, in their "copra cups" (the fibrous "outer" having previously been removed) and consume the whole lot with great relish. Obviously only top quality copra is good enough, and this the Seychelles deliver – for a number of good reasons.

Skilled workers halve the nuts with a practised swing of a machete, and lay them out in the sun to dry. These nut-halves are regularly turned over, so that they dry uniformly. The quality and taste of the fruit flesh can easily be impaired if this is not done properly. Ripe coconuts, because they are to a certain extent pre-dried already, are most suitable.

Generally, agile "pickers" shin up the palms, pluck the nuts from where they hang and throw them down into the ground, from where they can easily be gathered. This rationalisation of the harvesting process is certainly useful, especially on the immense plantations of the Philippines, Malaysia and Sri Lanka. The one small problem is that only a coconut which has dislodged itself, will be fully ripe. And this is where the Seychelles' palms come into their own: they possess that highly desirable attribute of always being "right on time", and the timely shedding of their fruit provides the best set of conditions for a good "copra cup". Much to the benefit of the export trade balance...

sarily upwards. The key export, copra (production has been at about 3,000 tons annually, in the last years) is a pretty sure bet, because of the constant high quality.

Cinnamon, which has been the other pillar of support for exports, has been badly affected by a fluctuating world market. Cinnamon rind production fell steeply, from

Cross section of a coconut

1,300 tons in 1973, to just under 400 tons in 1981, after having exceeded the value of copra production during the 60's, when the South-East Asian countries experienced production difficulties brought on by wars in that region. Additionally, decades of over exploitation led to the untimely demise of the huge cinnamon trees which had been shorne of their bark. As luck would have it though, a little bird saved the day for the cinnamon trade: thanks to the mynah bird, the seeds of the cinnamon were distributed over the whole of the island, and now both lone, and little clusters of "wild" cinnamon trees have grown up. In other words, cinnamon is no longer a plantation crop and it has become rather a painstaking task collecting and drying it. Periodically, oil is distilled from the cinnamon tree's leaves, but synthetic products and depressed prices have meant that this trade has all but lost its commercial significance for the Seychelles.

In past years vanilla was the third most important of the Seychelles' cash crops, with a maximum production figure of 70 tons annually having been achieved around the turn of the century, bringing in 50,000 rupees per ton. It was a relatively short-lived enterprise, however, (market prices had dropped within a short while) and, to cap it all, in the recent past a fungus, which has so far resisted all efforts to combat it, has more or less put the lid on vanilla production.

But, a little star has risen on the horizon: tea. Domestic requirements can, to all intents and purposes, already be satisfied from what is yielded by the plantation which was started in 1962 on the Forét Noir road in the highlands of Mahé. This road connects Victoria with Port Glaud. As only selected seedlings of top quality strains were used, the Seychelles tea has already been able to gain a name for itself in certain export markets; apart from regular tea, a cinnamon-flavoured variety is also produced. Trips to the so-called "tea factory" on the above-mentioned road, are one of the favoured excursions, and something out of the ordinary for the visitor.

In the past, efforts have been made to introduce other tropical cash crops and thereby strengthen the Seychelles' economic basis. In practice, it turned out that neither coffee, cocoa, cardamom nor cotton production could assert itself in the face of competition, especially that of the American producers.

That the production of pepper and nutmeg on the islands was stifled in its infancy, is a tragic tale for the telling: a "spice garden" had been planted, in 1771, in which cinnamon, pepper and nutmeg were doing quite nicely. But then in 1780 the Frenchman in charge of the gardens, a M. de Romainville, noticed an unidentified fleet of ships approaching and, fearing they were British men 'o'war, and not wanting the precious plantation to fall into enemy hands, he had it burned to the ground. (A practice which the Dutch were fond of, in Malacca, but an act perpetrated by others too, in those days.) Can you imagine the chagrin of the man when he realised that they were, in fact, his own lads! Only the robust cinnamon trees survived the "ordeal by the fire", thereby setting the stage for the production of cinnamon, in later years.

Vegetable production has, over the years been steadily increased, and the range of produce varies, according to the season (= monsoon period). Articles with which we are familiar, such as tomatos, cabbages and aubergines are cultivated, as well as the indigenous "patole", pumpkin, yam and manioc. Don't be fooled by the fact that the Saturday market in Victoria is chock-a-block full – domestic production can hardly meet the needs of the home market.

Fruit, on the other hand, is in plentiful supply: the generous range of tropical fruits which you will find so agreeable to partake of at any time between breakfast and your evening cocktails, includes bananas, pineapples, passion fruit and citrus fruits, mangos and papayas. The delights of the breadfruit and jackfruit tree seem to be more to the taste of the locals – for cooking purposes.

The lack of adequate pasture land has restricted attempts to rear cattle. You'll see a cow grazing, now and again, but that's about the state of things in respect of milk and beef production. Pig and fowl rearing has, in contrast, made good commercial headway on the islands.

If there's a lack of home-produced meat, there's certainly an over-abundance of fish available in the waters of the Seychelles, although the methods employed to harvest this bounty from the sea are more often of a traditional rather than a modern, industrial nature. Ships which load stocks of fish from the deep-freeze sheds are increasingly often to be seen in or just off Victoria harbour, but the fishing fleets, mainly of Eastern or Far-Eastern nations, can equally often be sighted within the now increased 200 nautical mile fishing zone. The initiative to intensify fishery activities on their own behalf, has now been taken.

The task of attracting or developing new industries is a thankless one, due mainly to the fact that there is an absolute lack of the necessary raw materials. And so energies have, so far, been channelled mainly into activities like ship and boat repairs, or the wood and metalwork trades – not to mention the manufacture of cigarettes or the brewing of beer. But again, heads have been put together, to come up with new ideas for creating more jobs and wealth. A – sadly – not terribly labour-intensive product has almost stealthily edged itself into the position of being one of the Seychelles' top currency earners: the postage stamp. These equally interesting as tastefully designed "bits of paper" trumpet word of the Seychelles, out into the big wide world, simultaneously bringing in more of the much-needed foreign exchange than say, such mundane things like guano or cinnamon.

Tourism: Currency Earner and Problem Child No. 1

In terms of tourism, the Seychelles is a late starter but, for that, its rise has been meteoric – and the first-hand experience of that well-known fact, that "what goes up, must come down", has been a bitter lesson for the learning.

As the tourist industry began to experience "golden days" in Europe, at the beginning of the 70's – within Europe and to holiday destinations abroad – the Seychelles were just a little unknown group of islands on the tourist's map of the world. Those visitors who came to enjoy the beauties of this neck of the woods were to be counted in their hundreds rather than thousands, and tended to be the more well-off globetrotters who would lay anchor in the harbour at Victoria, the capital.

Things changed almost overnight as, in 1972, the islands suddenly became accessible by air and not just via an extended sea voyage. Almost as if in anticipation of what was to follow the islands' then pending independence, declared in 1976, Britain had erected an international airport on Mahé, and handed it over as a sort of birthday present to the young republic. During 1972, 15,000 visitors arrived on these shores, and this marked the beginning of a rising tide of tourists, which culminated in a maximum figure, so far, of 80,000 visitors during 1979.

And everything seemed to be going so well: hotels were built, streets modernized or newly laid, personnel and supply problems mastered, often in the most ingeniously unconventional way. And the tourists, generally a pretty select crowd, came, saw and marvelled at this newly-discovered holiday paradise. But there was the old fly in the ointment which, in those early and you might say euphoric days, was either overlooked or made provision for and tucked away, under the heading of "neighbourliness". It soon grew however into a source of discontent for guests and potential visitors: the imbalance between (rising) prices and (declining) services the origins of which were to be traced back to a displacement of social values, and tensions, most noticeable in the service sector. Fishermen and agricultural workers who had downed tools and hot-footed it into town in order to get themselves better paid jobs and climb up the social ladder, also fell victim to the age-old sin of envy, and increasingly considered themselves hard done by in comparison with the more well-heeled tourists. And the fact that, because of the increasing number of visitors, not only the number of jobs increased, but prices took a healthy leap forward too-including those of the basic items which the Seychellois themselves had to buy – only served to fuel the fire of their discontent.

And then, when increasing wage costs and import duties sent prices (including those of the so-called "extras", such as taxi fares and a drink at the bar) rocketing, the thus far flourishing, "quality" tourist market nose-dived. The decline of the tourist market was also due, in part, to political unrest on the Seychelles, and the economic difficulties experienced by the industrialised nations – whence came the tourist. The admirable 1979 tourist count had fallen by half by 1982, to about 40,000.

And so the government stepped in. Tourism, and the considerable influence it had on the economy (employment, foreign income) was too golden a goose to just allow to flounder about. Selected hotels were bought up, refurbished, and a uniform and market-oriented price structure established; new partners – to promote tourism – were found; the new Air Seychelles enterprise was granted direct flight routes to and from Europe; and the problem of the irritating cost of those little "extras" was also dealt with, in consequence of which the price (Autumn '73) of a whisky (cognac or vodka), at the bar of the Barbarons Beach Hotel, stood at just 10 rupees – i. e. only half of what it would have knocked you back at the beginning of the year. The effect of the influence, yea pressure even, exerted by officialdom – and indeed the good example set by them – on those who determine prices on the islands, is unmistakeable: the 100 rupees airport tax which so many visitors found so annoyingly high, has simply been waived.

The results of all the measures taken were soon noticeable: in 1983 the tourist count had again risen to 55,000, the Germans nosing the French out of their position of being "most numerous visitors". That doesn't mean that the Seychelles, like some Spanish islands, are firmly in the hands of the German tourist: of the total, Germans represent about 17%, and of the total of visitors from Europe, they represent less than one quarter.

The principal tourist destination is – and how could it be any different? – the main island, Mahé, which of all the islands, has the largest hotels and consequently the most rooms/

beds to offer. But then, it is a shame, really, that only a very small proportion of holidaymakers spend their time on one or other of the smaller islands, such as Praslin or La Digue, or Bird or Denis Island. The first two are granite islands and are typically beautiful examples of the dream holiday the Seychelles can offer; the two latter are the only two coral islands of the archipelago which are fairly easily accessible from Mahé.

The Seychelles, the Gourmet and the Gourmand

When Adam nibbled at that fateful apple in the Garden of Eden, that was it. No more paradise for us. We have to content ourselves nowadays with the Seychelles where, according to what the locals say, things are not as they were in Eden. "He who partakes of the breadfruit shall indeed return one day to the paradise islands of the Seychelles." You'll note that there is no reference to sin, although there are one or two things, both on land and in the sea, for which one might be tempted to sin, just a little, perhaps.

Creative and imaginative – both words could be used to describe the Seychelles cook and indeed the rare and tasteful dishes he prepares from the fruits of this fertile tropical soil, as well as those he creates from the freshly-caught treasures of the sea. Don't be afraid to try something new, even if you aren't acquainted with all the ingredients. You'll find the essence of the Seychelles' Creole cuisine to be "artistry" resulting from French cooking harmonizing with the various influences of Chinese, African and English culinary traditions. That most of the menus will reflect basically French dishes is not surprising, as it was, after all, the French who first settled here, in number, over 200 years ago. The Indian influence has provided an increased adeptness with spices, especially cinnamon, vanilla, pepper and ginger, as well as the taste for hot curries. The immigrants from the African mainland brought with them their expertise in the preparation of dishes featuring tropical fruits and vegetables, of which the breadfruit, yams, pumpkins and cassava are noteworthy. The habit of taking afternoon tea is a legacy of British rule – exported by them to all their colonial possessions – and is widespread. It is also not unknown amongst the Seychellois, to partake of the traditionally English breakfast of ham 'n' eggs – especially of a Sunday morning.

The kingpin of Seychelles cooking is fish – no doubt about it. You get it grilled, baked, roasted or boiled and always or course, fresh and of the best quality. Tons of fish are to be found in the waters off these fair isles; tons of them and almost countless numbers of different varieties even. Should you like to see some of them, then a trip to the market, in Victoria, will be entertaining. Either that or go down to the beach and have a chat with the fishermen as they come off their boats. You'll be amazed at the sight of giant tuna and swordfish, kingfish and blue marlin, cordonnier, job, bourgeois, rouget, vieille, sharks, small and large mussels as well as delicacies such as crawfish – quite a bit different to herrings, place, cod and jellied eels!

Some tips here, now, for the fish freaks, which you on no account should miss: grilled tuna or swordfish steaks; savoury tuna fish with assorted herbs and cloves, or in a coconut marinade; grilled bourgeois with ginger, onions and garlic; braised fish chunks (Rougaille de Poisson, Daube de Poisson) or any one of the oh so tasty, typically Creole fish curries as e. g., curried squid (Carry Zourrite), or Carry de Bonite and last but certainly not least, steamed fish in coconut palm or banana leaves (Maquereau Boucaner). And remember, if you see the dish "Kat-Kat de Bananas au Poisson" on the menu, it is one of the all-time favourites of the local dishes – an incomparable concoction of fish, plantain bananas and coconut milk. Further specialities are: stuffed mussels (Palourdes Farcies) and a soup of tiny little mussels, called Soupe de Tec-Tec – tasty, tasty.

Fruit and vegetables here are extremely colourful, therefore pleasing to the eye, and a veritable delight to the taste buds. They form the "other" and equally important "half" of Seychelles cuisine, and are always skillfully prepared, dressed and served in the form of refreshing salads, dainty "chatinis" (shredded fruit and vegetable assortment, fried in oil), or "daubes" (fruit cooked in coconut milk). About the most popular single item, with practically everybody, is the banana, of which there are a couple of dozen varieties – ranging from the smaller, sweeter ones to record breaking specimens measuring about 2 ft. Next to the plantain (cooking banana – bananas St. Jacques), the sweet potato (patate douce) and the breadfruit, which can weigh 6 lbs. or more (fruits à pain), are the staple foods of the islanders. These and rice that is. They can, just like our potato (seems to have lost its lustre somehow), be deep-fried or boiled. Flour, made from the high-starch fruits, is used in baking the popular flat breads and pancakes such as e. g. the gallette, pain-pain or moucate.

Certainly unforgettable, almost a sensual delight: the tantalizing aroma of fresh mangos, pineapples, papayas, guavas, melons, limes, coconuts, golden apples (fruit ci tèrre) and in fact, that of a whole host of other fruits as well – whether you discover them in salads, in sweets, as such to refresh you, or as an entrée. Perhaps you'll be amongst the lucky few visitors who experience one of the most renowned dessert delicacies that the islands have to offer: the sweet jelly of a not quite ripe co-co-de-mer, which is the world's largest and heaviest "seed" and grows on Praslin. Another of the tasty dishes "fit for a king" which the Seychelles have to offer and you should try while you're here, even if you aren't terribly well-heeled, is the "millionaire's salad". It has the fact that a whole palmiste palm has to be felled, in order to get the delicate palm heart, to thank for its name.

You are indeed a gourmet, and courageous too, if trepidation does not accompany your approach to those of the locals' traditional titbits which owe their place on the menu to times when meat imports from South Africa were either a cause for celebration, or anyway too expensive. When the menu reads "Carry de Chauce Souris" or a dish is purported to be of "flying fox", you can rest assured that you are going to be served up something with the meat of the indigenous variety of bat (wing span can reach 3 ft.) in it. "Fricassee d'Oeufs d'Oiseaux" and "Carry Coco d'Oeufs d'Oiseaux" contain the eggs of various of the sorts of terns which breed in their hundreds of thousands on some of the islands.

It can't be denied: turtle meat tastes good. For a long time these animals provided practically the only source of meat on the more remote islands, but nowadays the turtle is a protexted species, the season and catch quotas strictly limited by the government and even then only the male specimens may be taken. In consequence, turtle meat will not usually be served, even on special occasions – but perhaps on very special ones. Perhaps the most spectacular of all the Seychelles' dishes-cum-ceremonies is one which you, in all probability, will not be party to.

And with good reason: the recipe prescribes that the meat of one whole turtle be separated whole from the shell and then heated up for some hours in an over-sized, natural cooking pot, over a slow fire until done. 200 years ago, back in the days of the early settlers and pirates, this dish would have had its place and provided them the necessary nutrition. In view of the fact that everyone is well-aware that turtles are nowhere near plentiful, and conservation is the order of the day, beef, pork or fowl dishes, which don't taste the same but are every bit as good and nourishing, are more in keeping. And these meats are often prepared in the form of ragouts, fricassees or hot curries, together with the famous "Riz Creole" – a savoury dish made of rice with ginger, onions, garlic and other vegetables. Try "Carry de Boeuf Riz Creole" or "Carry de Poulet au Coco Riz Creole", you won't be disappointed.

Hot spices are often employed in Creole cooking – highly spiced food is good for you in the tropics. But then you also have to know how to put out that fire in your mouth, and amongst the best remedies are the delicious sweet dishes the Seychelles' cuisine has to offer: cakes containing coconut such as "Gateau Coco", "Tarte au Coco", or cakes made of sweet potato with a vanilla sauce, "Gateau de Patate Sauce Vanille"; or coconut pudding, "Flan Coco"; crystallized bananas or a compote of any of a number of exotic fruits and, above all else, such delicious specialities as "Nougat Coco" or "Fondant au Coco".

The Number One thirst quenchers are drinks containing lemon juice, and mixed fruit drinks containing pineapple, guava, mango, passion fruit or lime juice, not to mention the coconut and what comes out of it. A number of fermented fruit juices will get you going. These include: "calou", made from the fuice of the young coconut, or "bacca" which is pineapple, but resembles rum. One "calou" too many and you'll know what's meant by the word "pernicious". You'd be safer to stick to the imported, if somewhat more expensive wines or the old favourite, beer. Seybrew, the local ale, is a bit like its German equivalent and can be recommended. There's no shortage of tea, it's an excellent thirst-quencher, locally grown and a makes for a quality "cuppa".

Daube de Poisson
(Stewed fish) 4 portions.
2 lbs. bourgeois, vieille or similar fish / 1 onion / 1 tomato / 2 to 3 cloves of garlic / fresh ginger root / oil, flour / salt, pepper, thyme, tomato puree.

Cut the fish into 1 inch cubes, roll in flour and then deep fry. Put to one side. Peel onion and cut into slices; slice tomato. Peel garlic and ginger; crush the garlic and grate the ginger.
Heat some oil in a frying pan, add onion and tomato; cover, fry lightly then add some water and allow to simmer. Add the deep-fried fish, tomato puree, garlic, ginger and thyme. Season to taste and stew for 15–20 minutes. Serve hot, with rice and salad or chatini.

Chatini de Cocos
4 portions.
2 whole coconuts or 1 lb. of grated coconut / 1 onion / 3 fresh peppermint leaves / pinch of allspice / juice of one lemon or lime / 1 sachet of saffron / salt, pepper and oil.

Crack the coconut and grate the fruit flesh. Peel the onion and cut into strips. Finely chop the peppermint leaves. Heat some oil in a casserole dish, brown the onions and add the saffron. Add the grated coconut and allspice. Season with salt, pepper and the chopped peppermint. Stew for 4 or 5 minutes, stirring regularly. Remove from heat and add lemon or lime juice.

Nougat Coco
12 ozs. grated coconut / 12 ozs. sugar / 1/3 pint of water / 2 fl. ozs. oil / pulp of one vanilla pod / grated nutmeg.

Add the sugar to the water in a pot, allow to dissolve, then bring to boil. Throw in the grated coconut and simmer gently, stirring the while, until the mixture turns a mid-brown colour (stay with it!) Remove from heat and season with the vanilla and nutmeg. Pour the mixture onto an oiled tray and spread flat. Allow to stand for a least two hours, then cut into inch sqares and serve as "petits fours".

Entertainment

As is beauty, so is the wide scope of entertainment the islands offer you – in the eye of the beholder.

On the one hand it will very much depend on what you expect to find to amuse and entertain you during your stay here. If you have it in mind to go out during the evenings, and go on a pub-crawl (or similar), or seek out numerous night spots to go dancing and let your hair down, you'll doubtless soon find the thin end of the wedge in your hand.

On the other hand, it depends also on what it is that you consider to be entertainment. Sure, yours and the other hotels offer a programme including music and dance, but within a week or two that will have been more than enough of a good thing for you, and you'll be ready for a bit of a change. If you're lucky, you'll have the chance to attend either a "camtole-show" or a "sega-cabaret" – music, song and dance à la Creole. (You'll find Jocelyn Perreau, a Mauritian who is married to a Seychellois, a first class entertainer.) Looking around, you'll find that it's the hotels which offer most of the night-time entertainment, e. g. the Equator Hotel is acclaimed by visitors and locals as the undisputed No. 1 disco spot. Then, every now and again, a fashion show will be staged, an exhibition of ceramics or other arts and crafts will be put on, and a whirlwind round of barbecues organized. And that will be about it.

So far, let it be said, it's been Mahé that has been referred to. The remaining islands and their hotels offer idyllic peace and seclusion for those who find they don't need to travel all this way for what they have enough of at home already.

P.S.: If you include an evening dining out in a refined atmosphere under the heading of "entertainment", then you will find your taste catered for. Apart from one or two of the hotels, there are a handful of restaurants which offer excellent Creole or international specialities, and justify the renown they enjoy. The "Marie-Antoinette" offers Creole cuisine, and "La Scala" and "Suisse Restaurant" (all in Victoria) are musts. On Praslin, your attention should be directed towards the "Chateau de Feuilles". The quality, style and refinement of these establishments is reflected in the cuisine as much as in the size of the accompanying bill. Every now and again management will change or the chef will leave, so inform yourself as to what and who is still "in" and/or "on", and what's new.

Seychelles Rhythms

The Seychellois love music, rhythm, and dancing. As in those times, some 200 years ago, when the slave was just a commodity, the music made here still reveals that selfsame, spirited joyfullness, together with a wistful longing to forget. To this day, the African ingredient in the make-up of the Seychellois' mentality has predominated over the cultural and intellectual influence provided by the French, who firmly made their mark on the Creole language, as spoken here.

The duality of the cultural heritage is reflected in the music of the islands: moutia and séga are musical forms, of African origin, which belong to the daily routine and are also popular at dances or festive occasions. The moutia counts as the cornerstone of Seychelles music: a ritual prayer turned into a worksong by the slaves. The accompanying rhythmic dance routine gives physical expression to sorrow, hope and aspiration.

Popularly, the moutia will take place in the shadowy light of a bonfire, preferably at full moon, and the men and women take turns at preforming the age-old routines to the accompaniment of a punctuating rhythm beaten out on a big round drum. The séga is pretty similar to the moutia, differing from the Mauritian version, in that the percussion instrument is not of the same type: the pounding beat is hammered out on the hollowed-out trunk of a palm tree.

An intrinsically French melody and dance tradition has also been handed down, alongside the musical forms emanating from Africa, viz: the contredanse. It came with the French settlers, can today be seen as a cross between a waltz, polka and a berliner and is generally performed by a camtole band which usually comprises fiddle, accordeon, banjo and drums. You can't beat it as all-round good-time music and it's consequently always on the agenda at weddings or other family celebrations.

Out and About, in and on the Seychelles

After all the things you'll have read about the Seychelles, the time has come to see, feel and hear as many of the marvels as time and opportunity will allow. Should Mahé be your "base", then you'll have no trouble getting "out and about, in and on the Seychelles."

Mahé is the largest of the archipelago's islands, and therefore offers the most things to get your keen, willing fresh tourist teeth into. Mahé is also the crossroads of air and sea traffic for the region, and so you have the best opportunities for getting to the other islands on your doorstep. Do travel around because only then will you get a real and proper impression of the diverse beauty and magnificence of this group of islands.

An asessment of the island in terms of navigable streets and highways, reveals a course measuring some 15 miles (north-south) by all of 3 miles (east-west). You can complete the course in well under a day, and will find that you needn't have notched up more than say 70 miles in your hire-car. But covering the island in this way means that you only see two of the five different types of terrain and scenery, and that in passing, and you wouldn't have had any time to enjoy either stopping off at some of the picturesque little villages, taking in the view from any of a number of vantage points or to relax a little on some of the beautiful beaches down in the south.

Bus tours offered by the local operators include commentaries in English, and they're worthwhile. As the north Mahé tours will take in the botanical garden and orchid garden, the museum in Victoria as well as the aquarium at Glacis and the island's tea plantation, the commentaries are most helpful and also stimulating. A south Mahé tour comes more under the heading of "panoramic views", and takes you through some beautiful parts of the southerly, eastern and western coasts as well as into the island's interior. That a bus tour won't (normally) include some of the most "typical of the Seychelles" beaches which Mahé has to offer, of which Anse Intendance is the prime example, has to be rectified in that you "go it alone".

And there are three charming ways of going about it. The choice is yours:

Car hire has developed into a good business on Mahé, and you can hire anything from a mini to a mercedes, although English and Japanese models are most commonly available (automatics are as good as nonexistent). The mini-moke is about the most popular item and you can have a lot of fun in one, with the hood down, letting the wind take your hair. Comfort, of course, in one of these things, is a relatively low-key consideration. If it happens that you get caught in a sudden rain shower, don't bother to try and hastily fix up the hood: before you get it up you'll be drenched anyway, and the shower will be over too. Much better to take it in your stride, and rely on the

warm wind, blowing past you as you drive, to dry you out again in a twinkling.

Mahé and Praslin are the only islands on which you can hire cars, and are as well the only islands with any road network to speak of. As a rule the roads are asphalted and are designated as main roads, which term refers more to the extent of the network than the significance of the roads themselves. If, for example, you're out and about on the west coast, you'll needs must navigate the road between Anse Boileau and Grande Anse Village, a road in tune with the description "secondary", being a string of potholes held together by the semblance of a made up road. You really do have to navigate well. In fairness, they are about the job of seeing to it.

On the whole the roads don't induce one to speed, a fact with won't bother you as holidaymaker who wants to look around and enjoy the scenery. On the open road the speed limit is 40 mph; in built up areas and in Victoria itself, you drive at a maximum speed of 25 mph. which is also the limit, generally, on Praslin.

In the Seychelles you drive on the left. Anyone not used to this might find it strange at first but will soon get used to the traffic system. More taxing is the inadequate signposting of the roads. So, always carry a good roadmap with you (one is included with this guide). The help of the policeman is always at hand, courtesy of the many police stations which you will find, often situated at crossroads, intersections etc. Not surprisingly, they are helpful and well-informed. Case in point: the road to the above-mentioned beach at Anse Intendance, branches off at Quatre Bornes, opposite the police station there. So far, so good. The turn off for Anse Intendance is not signposted, and it's left up to you to figure it out with whatever help your map happens to be to you.

In case "following your nose" is something that past experience has suggested you leave out, hire a car plus driver, instead – its regular practice. Either that or consider an alternative method of getting about. One of which would be, our second suggestion:

Taxi tours allow you the same degree of mobility, include a driver who will know the island like the back of his hand, don't involve any red tape at all and can be booked for as long or short a haul as tickles your fancy. Agreeing a price shouldn't prove difficult either, as a fixed scale of charges, relating to point to point hirings, has been laid down by the government. Your hotel will be fully informed and can therefore put you in the picture. There's obviously a little room for the driver to manoeuvre, and charge for waiting time, but you'll be able to tell if the driver wants to take you for a ride of the sort you can do without – and there are any number of fixed-price standard drives.

The public bus service of the S.P.T.C. (Seychelles Public Transport Corporation) represents our third, and by no means meanest, suggestion of possible ways of discovering Mahé under your own steam. It's certainly the cheapest method: the bus fare, for rides outside of urban Victoria, is 50 cents per fare stage, which, in this case means per stop, and if you pay your full 50 cents per stop for a "bus route" roundtrip of the whole island, you won't have shelled out more than 20 rupees. A total of 24 separate bus routes serve Victoria and the various outlying villages, covering all the coastal roads and some services cut across the width of the island, through the highlands. And so it's easy to get to any and all of the interesting sights and beaches, including those, which like Anse Intendance are off the beaten track and require a bit of a walk despite the bus service – an appearance at Anse Intendance = 20 minutes on foot. 4 S.P.T.C. bus routes run on Praslin too.

There is no fixed timetable, but the buses do run from 5:30 am to 7 o'clock in the evening during the week; buses on some of the longer runs, on Mahé, stop running a bit earlier. Enquire at your hotel as to what time, approximately (no time table, tropical country: manana), the last buses run, whether late afternoon or evening, from e.g. Port Glaud, Takamaka or Bel Ombre, back to Victoria or wherever (presumably your hotel) you want to go to. And spare a thought for the fact that as traffic drives on the left, the bus stop you want will be to your left hand, when looking in the direction you want.

Boat tours, when you're on holiday in a paradise consisting of lots of islands, are as important, if not more so, than excursions and sightseeing trips on land.

You have lots of possible sea rides to choose from, from Mahé. For a start there's the Ste. Anne Marine National Park, right in front of Victoria's front door (so to speak).
It encompasses the lush coral beds around the islands of St. Anne, Cerf, Moyenne, Cachée, Round and Long Island. Excursions in glass-bottomed boats enable you to view the wonders of the underwater world amongst the coral; snorkelers are in their element here. Many of the tours from Victoria are whole-day tours, including landings on Moyenne, Round and/or Cerf.

Further trips, to islands in Mahé's immediate vicinity, will take you to Therese and Silhouette; farther destinations offered, show the bird island of Aride and also Praslin and La Digue. Or, what about a day's fishing, out in a boat? And an afternoon mini-cruise around north Mahé, during which you'll witness an impressive sunset, is worth every penny.

The route from Praslin to La Digue is plied by two ferries, the "Lady Mary II" and the "Ideal", and this crossing takes about half an hour (outward journey am., return pm.). Excursions to the bird island of Cousin, as well as to the Curieuse National Park (in which lies the island to which the park owes its name) are also possible from Praslin.

Island Hopping, in the trim little craft belonging to Air Seychelles, is one of the most charming and exhilarating ways of getting to know this island domain of the Seychelles – the birds eye view is breathtaking to experience. The ocean is alive, showing hundreds of different and changing, sparkling iridescent hues of colour for the eye to marvel at: the sea varies from greens to blues, the coral banks from yellow-brown to green. Dotted about in the wide expanse of the ocean, the islands appear like blobs of strong green colour encircled by a strip of yellow-coloured sand and surrounded by a silver "halo" – the sea breaking on the coral reefs. This sight alone makes a flight-excursion so desirable a distraction. The choice of flight "hops" includes day trips to Frégate and Praslin, also in combination with a visit to La Digue, air-time each way being about 15 minutes, and an excursion "hop" to Bird Island lasting 40 minutes each way. If you had anyway planned your holiday to include a few days on Bird or Denis Island (which, in retrospect, you might well come to regard as the high-spot of your "Seychelles experience"), then a substantial "island hop" will already be included in the price of the holiday. A few tips in respect of bookings: if you want to hire a car during the main season (July/August, mid-December/mid-January), you should make provision for this when making the original booking (flight, hotel etc.) at your travel agency. On the spot hirings (on the Seychelles) aren't cheaper, because a uniform rate-scale is in force, and you are restricted to what's available at that time. You might only get a model you didn't want.

One can arrange to spend several days on the islands of Praslin and La Digue, Bird and Denis Island as well as on Moyenne and Poivre Island/Amirantes. The latter two islands have only minimal capacity of 2 and 4 double rooms respectively and you get to Poivre courtesy of a 20 hour sail. Arranging to spend some time on one of the other islands is best sorted out together with your original booking at your travel agency back home. Not that it's not possible to arrange these visits through a travel agent on Mahé, but you might either have difficulty in getting any discount on your hotel bill for days you don't spend there or, if you extend the duration of your holiday, you might well experience real problems trying to re-arrange your flight departure date.

What's That in "Creole"?

Possessing a good command of the English language doesn't necessarily mean that you'll be able to converse all that well with the locals, and so you'll find a few phrases of Creole very useful.

Knowing a bit of French is very helpful, because Creole is a phonetic derivation of that language, and similar versions of it are spoken in regions in which French influence has been dominant e. g. Mauritius, Martinique or New Orleans. The less accented syllables of the original French words have been run together, and soft sounds often turned into harder ones as, e. g. "chaise" (chair) into "sez".

When trying out your linguistic expertise, try to pronounce every syllable clearly and not to "swallow" any of them.

Forms of Address

Good morning	Bonzoor
Good evening	Bonzwar
Goodbye	Orrevwahr
How are you?	Comman cava?
What's happening?	Ki i deer?
I'm fine, thankyou	Mon bien, mersi
What's your name?	Comman ou appelay?
My name is George	Mon appel George
Are you French?	Ou Fransay?
Swiss?	Swiss?
English? Seychellois?	Anglay? Sayselwah?
No, I'm German	Non, mon Alman

Out and about

What time does the 'plane leave, please?	Caylair avvion ee Kitai, sivooplay?
Is it far?	Ee looenne?
Is it near?	Ee pray?
Is this our bus?	Sa noo bis? Noo bis sa?
Is this our boat?	Sa noo batto? Noo batto sa?
Are we going to Victoria?	Noo pay al Victoria?
Are you going to Praslin?	Oo pay al Praslin?
Yes, we are going to Victoria.	We, noo pay al Victoria.
No, I'm not going to Praslin.	Non, mon par pay al Praslin.

Enquiries

Where is... please?	Oli... silvooplay?
the bank	Labank
the market	bazaar
the bar	bar
my room	mon lasanm
my luggage	mon bagaz
my key	mon laclay
Where are you?	Oli oo?
Here I am.	La mon la.
Where are we now?	Kotay noo ettay la?
Where do you live?	Kotay oo restay?

Some Phrases

Excuse me, can I have a light, please?	Eskis mwan, oo annan difay silvooplay?
What time is it, please?	Kellair ee ettay silvooplay?
What's today's date?	Key dat ozzordee?
What time does the bar close?	Kellair bar ee fermen?
Can I use the 'phone, please?	Mon kappa servi telefonn, silvooplay?
Would you like to dance?	Oolay dansay?
Can you do the sega?	Oo kappa dansay sega?
Yes I can. How about you?	We mon kappa. Bay oo?
Let's dance this sega.	Annoo dansay sa sega.
Would you like a drink?	Ooellay en bwar?
Can I have a beer, please?	Mon kappa ganny en labeer, silvooplay?
I'm tired.	Mon fatigay.
I'm going to sleep.	Mon pay al dormi.
How much is this shell?	Conbyen sa cocki?
How much do I owe you?	Conbyen mon dwa oo?
This is beautiful.	Sa ee tzoli.
This beach is beautiful.	Sa lans ee tzoli.
What's the name of this beach?	Commanyer sa lans ee appellay?
What do you call this fish?	Komanyer sa pwasson ee appellay?

Sports... Sport

As islands are known, commonly, to be surrounded by lots of water, you can expect to have a real whale of a time enjoying every imaginable sort of watersport. The Seychelles are no exception, and specific, organized facilities offered vary from island to island. What the various hotels offer, depends also on their location.

Windsurfing has established itself as a popular indulgence here. The majority of the hotels on Mahé, Praslin and Denis islands cater for not only the competent sportsman, but can offer instruction for the beginner too. On the beach at Beau Vallon Bay, on Mahé, you also find "schools" – not connected with any hotel – which will impart the necessary skills to you: the "Beau Vallon Bay Water Sports Centre", and "Seychelles Windsurfing Ltd." – both are affiliated to European water sports associations.

If you don't want to keep falling off your board because of either the high winds or rough water, or indeed, from time to time, have to pass up the opportunity completely, then note the following: the southeast trade winds blow from May to October, during which time the leeward side of the islands (e. g. on Mahé, the north-west and west coast) are your best bet; when the north-west monsoon is going through its paces, in the period November to April, better surfing conditions are found on the east coast where you will, however, find the choice of hotels limited in comparison with that of Beau Vallon Bay or Grande Anse.

Sailing. The above applies equally to this sport; appropriate facilities are offered by hotels on the northwest and east coasts of Mahé and the west and east coasts of Praslin. Yachts and sailing boats can be hired by the hour or day, at the Victoria Yacht Club. Associate membership can be arranged.

Water skiing is best when the water is fairly calm, and conditions are really only (ideally) suitable at Beau Vallon Bay, when the southeast trade wind blows, from May to October. The Beau Vallon Water Sports Centre can, however, arrange to oblige between November and April as well, wind and water conditions allowing.

Paragliding. Same as for waterskiing.

Snorkel Diving in the Seychelles is so much fun because, as the government enforces a strict policy of conservation and preservation (not only in respect of sea life), the coastal waters are teeming with life, allowing you the illusion that the waters from the coast to the banks of the offshore coral reefs are part of nothing less than one giant tropical aquarium. Above all, one should mention the Marine National Parks of Ste. Anne – off the capital, Victoria – and of Curieuse – off the northern coast of Praslin – as real eye openers for the underwater fan. Moreover, wind and water conditions allowing – and this depends upon either monsoon or trade wind abating a little – the waters of Mahé's west coast and those around the smaller islands off Praslin and La Digue have astounding subaquatic sights to offer. Hints as to good spots to explore can be extracted from hotel personnel and the diving centres which also hire out the boats to get to wherever…

Snorkelling is sport for anybody who can swim. All you need to do in the salt water which carries you so well, is to occasionally give a kick or two with your flippers, in order to propel yourself around to your hearts' content. And, together with a mask and a snorkel tube, a pair of flippers is all you need. You can buy this equipment at home, or in the appropriate shops in Mahé – or hire them out from your hotel or from a diving club.

Over 300 species of fish and more than 100 species of coral are happily at home in these pleasant waters, and you can see a good many of them whilst flopping about in the shallow waters amongst the reefs. A host of snails and mussels, exist here too, and they all – including the fish and coral – come under the protection of the government's preservation policy. Harpooning is prohibited and offenders punished.

It is wise to wear a T-shirt, even whilst snorkelling, to protect your skin against the strong sun.

Diving takes you even deeper (literally!) into Neptune's realm. This doesn't necessarily mean that divers only ever work at great depths, however. They also like to stay just beneath the surface so as to enjoy a wider picture of the undersea world in all its natural beauty.

You need to know what you're doing when you go diving, and all the knowledge you could want is available from diving schools such as the one at the Equator Residence Hotel, on the west coast (Mahé), or at the Coral Strand Hotel (Seychelles Underwater Centre) at Beau Vallon Bay (also Mahé). The course lasts several days and you are taught the theory, and are instructed in the practical aspects of diving and use of the equipment involved. You must be at least 16, fit, able to swim and have experience of snorkelling.

Ready to cater fully for the needs of either Gunga Din or divers of any degree of proficiency, are, apart from the already mentioned Seychelles Underwater Centre at Beau Vallon Bay: Tecnosub, in Victoria and Gregoire's Diving Centre, on La Digue; enquire as to facilities available on Praslin.

An impression of the variety and choice of diving spots/excursions available, here an extract from the weekly timetable of Gregoire's Diving Centre (La Digue). Some are whole-day, others half-day outings:

Big Sister (big rock) – Rock Severe – Ave Maria (little island) – Rock Segrim (large granite cliff) – Madame Pierre – the ile Cocos (little island) – Felicité and Marianne (larger islands) – Shark Rock – Caiman Rock – Ennerdale (sunken tanker, wreck).

At maximum depths of 70 feet, underwater visibility is often an amazing 50 yds. and more, and even in the channels etc. you are hardly ever bothered by tiresome currents. The best months for diving, November – May.

Deep-sea fishing is an up-and-coming pastime here. It's no secret that people have been landing blue, and black marlin, tuna, wahoo, barracuda and bonito in these parts for some time. Also, the Seychelles is one of three game zones for the dogtooth tuna (Gymnosarda unicolor), This specimen was officially

declared a game fish by the I. G. F. A. (International Game Fish Association) in 1975 and by the end of 1977, the laurels for having broken the world record (biggest fish landed) had gone to Denis Island five times.

The waters around the coral islands of Denis and Bird, though known to give shelter to a most remarkable variety of game fish both large and small, including the bonefish, spearfish and marlin, are still, as yet, relatively unexplored territory. That this region of the sea is close to the edge of the Seychelles Bank, where the seabed drops steeply down to a depth of 6,000 ft., influences much of what goes on here. In contrast, the waters covering the Seychelles Bank, in the centre of which are grouped the granite islands, are nowhere deeper than 230 ft. The waters are thus eminently suited to a traditional method of fishing engaged in by the Seychellois: angling (hook, line and sinker). Usually the catch includes fish of a variety of lovely colours with just as lovely Creole names such as bourgeois, vara-vara, dame berry and capitaine rouge.

You can book deep-sea fishing or angling tours in Mahé (good tours are offered by the Seychelles Marine Charter Association, at the harbour in Victoria), at various hotels in Praslin, La Digue and on both Denis and Bird islands, and these will usually also have all the necessary and appropriate equipment and boats.

Having to go and look for a place to hire a rod and line is work, so, keen angler, bring your own unless you intend to buy.

The months of November to April will bring more of a gleam to the deep-sea angler's eye than July and August, during which the south-east trade winds can whip up some troubled waters.

Sports (on land) are provided for mainly on Mahé but can't really compete with what the sea has to offer.

Tennis is played in the grounds of several of the hotels; some of the courts can be floodlit. Good players are often attracted to the "Tartan Court" of the Equator Residence Hotel.

Golfing facilities are based at the Reef Hotel (east coast) and at the Barbarons Beach Hotel (on the west coast) – guests of the latter play at the Beoliere Country Golf 9-hole "pitch and putt" course. The Reef Hotel Golf-Club is open to local residents as well as guests who wish to become associates.

Riding is a pastime to be engaged in whilst simultaneously enjoying the grounds of the Barbarons Estate, on the west coast. Rides through the wooded heights overlooking Barbarons and Anse Boileau, and through the old plantation, are a delight for experienced as well as novice riders.

Cycling is popular on Praslin and La Digue (tours are very pleasant). On Praslin the steep inclines in the Vallée de Mai area could provide you with quite enough exitement as the caliper brakes on your steed will often need to be applied. Rates are also steep (see the fold-out map section at rear).

Hiking is perhaps one of the last things you might have expected to be taking your time up with but, with a good stout pair of walking shoes, an extended "constitutional" through the heights and more mountainous areas of Mahé should put some hairs on your chest – and increase your wind.

The Victoria Trail will take you across and around the capital.

Trois Fréres they call the route, from Sans Souci, which will put you on nodding terms with many rare trees and plants and, weather permitting, allow you the pleasure of some distant and magnificent views over the islands off the coast. Should take about 3 hours.

The Anse Major Trail leads from Danzilles into the north-western portion of Mahé; here again many interesting specimens of trees, bushes and flowers are to be found.

Trail maps for the first two above-mentioned walks can be obtained from the Tourist Information Centre in Victoria.

Further sports, such as squash, badminton, mini-golf, table-tennis, croquet and boccia are possible at various hotels, and you are also invited to participate in sporting activities at Seychelles College.

Souvenirs, Souvenirs...

One souvenir that you should purchase as soon as possible after arriving, and that will serve you well: a wide, broad-brimmed hat fashioned from palm leaves, just like ones you see all the Seychellois wearing. This is better protection against the intensity of the sun's rays than any cream could be and will shade your head and neck admirably.

Baskets and table mats (also made of the same material) together with your hat, belong to those things that will travel back with you well, and won't weigh a lot. These and some of the batik or hand printed materials (also made up into light, airy beachwear), coral and mother of pearl jewellery of which a good selection is available in the better shops and boutiques in e. g. Independence Avenue, in the Victoria arcades and at Beau Vallon or in some of the hotel boutiques, are the "basics" to bring back with you.

If the additional weight you are collecting with each further souvenir doesn't bother you, then you might like to cast an eye over the goods on view in the Seychelles Home Industries sales and exhibition rooms – you'll find an ample selection of hand-crafted woodwork, shells, coconuts and palm articles to choose from. Something else that might also induce you to spend even your last few coppers (or more), is the selection of most attractive and artistically worked tortoiseshell items, be it in the shape of a bangle, or fashioned into cutlery or whatever. A word of warning: these tortoiseshell articles are made of tortoiseshell (hawksbill turtle) – and these animals enjoy the protection of the "Washington Convention". The import of all such items (even those made up partly of tortoiseshell) is prohibited by countries which subscribe to the convention. So, if the country you will be going back to has ratified the convention, then you might have the offending article(s) confiscated by customs on arrival, despite the fact that trade in articles made of the shell of these endangered animals is legal in the Seychelles themselves. **Your contribution** to the well-being of these animals would be **not to purchase** any such items.

Plenty of original souvenirs, which won't cause officialdom to become official (but perhaps be astounded), are available, such as e. g. the "jaws" of a shark. The street/beach traders smilingly offer them to you as an alternative set of dentures for granddad. Walking sticks, fashioned out of the backbone of sharks, are available in number in the souvenir shops in Independence Avenue between the Pirates' Arms Café and the Clock Tower in Victoria, The white coral and many shells also offered are certainly less "martial" in appearance, but remember that every piece sold means another item of marine life stolen from the reefs; another loss to nature. The principle applies to shells, coral and turtles alike: no demand – supply dwindles.

Ceramics (pottery work), exhibited at the Mamelle Pottery Centre, a mile south of Mahé, on the airport road, should be considered too. The Craft Centre, on Francis Rachel Street, opposite the "Cable and Wireless" building also has attractive items.

One agreeable way to remind both yourself, and your friends, of your time spent on the Seychelles, is to take back a collection of the spices (nicely bagged) which you can purchase from the Indian trader's shops around Victoria market, or indeed in the market itself. You can buy some of the locally-grown tea, to take back as well – in Victoria, direct from the "Tea Tavern" on the Sans Souci road, or you could leave it as late as the duty-free shop, on departure. Half pound and 2 oz. packs are available, so you can use up your remaining few rupees on them as opposed to spending them on cigarettes and spirits which cost as much here as in a supermarket.

The purchase of two other types of "special" Seychelles souvenirs require your specific attention: stamps are available, and there's a comprehensive selection of them at the philatelic counter in the main post office in Victoria; at a special counter you will find offered the more rare first day covers and "singles", some dating back a good few years and costing only a little more than the face value, i. e. good value. The other item referred to, perhaps the most sought-after souvenir the islands offer, but which also means spending a bit more money, is the renowned coco-de-mer. Nature has fashioned this fruit into as many variations of shape and form, as she (mother nature) allowed herself when fashioning "woman". You could procure for yourself either the complete, whether highly polished or in the natural state, item or articles fashioned from this nut-fruit (fruit bowl, vase etc.). Volume, and the weight (baggage) involved might well be a consideration here. Price will be another factor. The cricket ball sized, brown polished articles available at the booths opposite the post office in Victoria (and elsewhere) are not dwarf-versions of the real thing, but wooden replicas which are cleverly adorned with coconut husk.

Talking of replicas: quality models of fishing boats and historical sailing ships are available, though not cheap, at the La Marine workshops (Le Cap, on the eastern coastal road on Mahé, behind the Reef Hotel). Packed suitably for transit they can, without question, be entrusted to the airline for forwarding. Consider also the duty you will be asked to pay on the item, by customs, on arrival home.

A further suggestion as to souvenirs, if perhaps one of a more sophisticated nature, would be one of the works of art exhibited at the Galerie d'Art No. 1 (State House Avenue, Mahé Trading Building, Victoria). Both Seychellois, and foreign artists now resident, exhibit their works here including aquarels, graphic art and batik work. You can also get the addresses of the various artists, most of whom welcome a visit from a critical customer. Should you find the works to your taste, you'll also appreciate that there are some treasures on offer.

A final suggestion: Why not take home with you a little pouch of sand from each of the beaches you've visited. Whiter, finer stuff you won't find in this world.

Works of Art in Miniature

Most people, when they think of postage stamps from Indian Ocean island states, think first of philately's greatest historical rarity: the "Mauritius Blue". Well, neither the Seychelles, nor indeed any other country, can compete on this level. And how could they? At the time when the world's first gummed stamp – the famous "Penny Black" of 1840 – appeared, and when some short while later that unfortunate misprint of "Post Office", instead of "Post Paid" took place in Mauritius, the Seychelles were still being administered from Mauritius, and didn't issue any stamps of their own.

Well, the situation was rectified in 1890, and from this time on the Seychelles stamps have found favour amongst stamp collectors the world over, because of their rarity and the consequent increased value this gives them (especially true of the older issues). The point is this: at the turn of the century the population count of this country was pretty low, the amount of mail sent abroad correspondingly so, numbering not more than a handful of letters once or twice a month. Whenever Seychelles stamps are put up for auction – mainly in London – you can be sure that the bidding and the atmosphere will be competitive, and the proceeds for the seller, high.

The more recent issues of Seychelles postage stamps obviously don't fetch such amounts, but they are worth every penny you would pay for them. Any international "beauty contest", in which qualities such as choice of motif, artistic appeal and design or engraving or print quality were to be assessed, would be the richer for its "contestants" from the Seychelles, and they would have every chance of being amongst the prize winners. The stamps which have been produced in the last 15 years are picture-book representations of the Seychelles: giant tortoises and chameleons are depicted, coco-de-mer palms or wild vanilla seem to virtually grow out of the stamps; there are ox-carts lorries put to use as buses, sailing schooners and the Royal Yacht (to mark the occasion of HRH and Lady Dianas wedding); birds of the Seychelles, wild flowering plants and blossoming orchids, fish and turtles swimming and even the inauguration of "Seychelles Air's scheduled flight services".

To show the world the "true face of the Seychelles", is the task the postal authorities have set themselves, and they do it within the limits of five new issues of stamps per year. Wise move. Income from sales of these miniature works of art exceeds that generated by the coconut, not to mention cinnamon or what have you.

The stamps are a lovely little decorative embellishment of your postcards (or long letters) home.

Photo Tips

Getting your bag of photographic tricks together for a visit to the Seychelles requires no more preparation than for a trip to anywhere else. So, check your equipment make sure your batteries are functioning and take spare ones along too; you know that batteries which have been partly used and then been left can suddenly "die" on you, if they are suddenly put to "heavy duty" use again.

For general use on the islands you need only load your camera with the less sensitive film, e. g. 64 ASA/ISO = 19 DIN or 25 ASA/ISO = 15 DIN. The slower-speed films are suitable because of the good light conditions. However, when stepping out to places like the Vallée de Mai, on Praslin, the home of the coco-de-mer, then you'd be well-advised to use high-speed film, e. g. 200 ASA/ISO = 24 DIN or 400 ASA/ISO = 27 DIN. With this sort of high-speed film you can still "snap" to your heart's content, despite the lack of light caused by the dense roof of leaves way above your head. A real "prize" would be to get the rare black parrot in your sights (zoom or tele-lens fitted, granted).

Taking photographs in the light (and heat) of the midday equatorial

sun (almost vertically above you) can result in some disappointments. Close-up shots (portraits) can come out like this: a face with a couple of dark patches which would normally be the eyes. This is because the slight protrusion of the eyebrows casts sufficient shadow over those "orbs" that that is about what comes out: black orbs – unless of course, you use some flash to additionally illuminate your subject.

Photographs taken of beach scenes, where much of the picture background includes the light-coloured sand, can also turn out a disappointment, as the strength of the midday sun and the light reflecting properties of the sand can cause your exposure meter to give some false readings – false from the point of view of the resulting photographs. Normally, under-exposure will result from your meter reacting – because of the reflected light – as though there was more light, and so, setting your shutter speed and aperture accordingly. Adjusting the settings to get good definition and colour images of people, palm trees or the decorative granite cliffs, can result in the sand looking like the snow on Mount Everest.

This description is basically to give an understanding of the reason why professional photographers line up these (beach, sand) scenes and other motifs bathed in strong sunlight, between the hours of 7:30 a.m.–10:00 a.m. and 3:30 p.m.–6:00 p.m. The time from 11 in the morning to 2 in the afternoon is reserved for experiments – but you never know... If you take the advice, you'll have less wastage.

The heat is one of the worst enemies of the photographer. Better said, of his film – whether exposed or not. This doesn't mean, of course, that it will suddenly go off, but you need to do your utmost to protect your film from the heat. So, when you go on a trip, take only the film you'll need, not all your stock (an extra roll, in case, is always useful).

Remove used film from your camera and store it there where the rest of your stock should be, in a corner of your, presumably, cool air-conditioned hotel room. And in a plastic bag it will also be less likely to be affected by atmospheric humidity.

A different set of conditions governs the art of underwater colour photography. First of all, the deeper down you go, the more colours – apart from blue – are filtered out by the sea. To rectify this, you positively must work with a flash. Without a flash, and up to about 10 ft. down, photographs taken do portray the "underwater" atmosphere strikingly well (the clarity of the waters around Mahé, Praslin and La Digue allows good photos to be taken). And if you are particular about bringing out the true colours of the fish you'll be photographing, then there's no way round it: fix up the flash – whatever the depth.

From the sea, into the air. A hint again. This time for the proud owners of the fully automatic instruments, particularly those which have the "auto-focus" facility: the reason why your lovely shot out of the porthole (airplane or cruiser) didn't work, is because the autofocus is designed to focus on the next best solid object in line with the direction of the lens. And so, it will have focused, as sharply as possible, on the glass of the porthole or window through which you'd seen whatever magnificent sight – clouds, sea, islands – you'd seen, causing the object upon which you'd focused your intent, to become the out-of-focus subject of your discontent.

The Seychellois have nothing against being photographed, as a rule. They do, sometimes, take offence at not being asked first. All you needed to do was to point to your camera, indicate the request with a glance and all would have been well. The people here thank goodness, aren't in the habit of expecting gratuities for allowing themselves to be photographed – let alone expect modelling, fees. You might even cause offence by offering money. This doesn't mean that a child wouldn't accept a sweet or a picture postcard of where you come from, the men a foreign cigarette or the ladies a (suitably small) bottle of toilet water.

To come back to tips again: the lighter-coloured the background or surroundings (sky or light coloured hat etc.) of a dark-skinned subject you wish to photograph, the more untrue are the settings indicated by your exposure meter. Take the aperture stops down one or two points to correct this, i. e. f5.6 or f4 rather than f8 or, in the case of automatic cameras, make sure the respective correction facility is activated. One way to proceed, is to (temporarily) alter the film-speed dial on your camera, i. e. if you've got 25 ASA/15 DIN in, alter the film-speed indicator to 64 ASA/19 DIN. And even then, take a few shots, at different settings – just to be sure.

Should you run out of film, you can easily get standard material, at a price, from one of the three photographic dealers in Victoria. The boutiques in the hotels also, of course, offer the more popular-selling brands and formats.

Mahés Restaurants in Brief

"It may well be that French cuisine is excellent, Chinese food mouthwatering, and the use made of spices in Indian fare unparalleled... but just imagine a combination of all three and you get some idea of the delights of Creole cooking." (Taken from a book on food in the Seychelles.)

It's a relief to discover that most hotels in the Seychelles do not only feature "international" menus (whatever "international" might mean!) but also offer a great many traditional dishes as well.

Mahé boasts a fair number of restaurants and here, too, you'll be able to enjoy authentic and imaginative Creole cooking. They include:

The **Marie Antoinette**, St. Louis. This restaurant is located in a beautiful, old colonial villa, looks out over Victoria and can boast some of the most refined of Creole cooking.
La Perle Noire, Beau Vallon. Seafood in "rustic" surroundings.
Au Capitaine Rouge, Anse à la Mouche Guests sit in the open-air and enjoy the ideal setting of the restaurant in this beautiful bay. Seafood is the speciality of the house.
Juliana's, Anse à la Mouche. The restaurant looks out over the bay and itself enjoys a beautiful setting. Famous for its wonderful fish dishes and salads.
Sundown Restaurant, Port Glaud. A small beach restaurant offering some very imaginative dishes – especially grills "à la Creole".

La Sirene, Anse aux Poules Bleues. Another beach restaurant. Here you'll have a wonderful view of the coast and hills. Specialities include "chauve-souris" (bat).
Carefree, Anse aux Pins. This is a small, quite simple restaurant where you can enjoy tasty Creole dishes. Not far from the airport.

Asian and European styles of cooking are also quite well represented. Restaurants to be recommended include:

Chinese
The Mandarin, Victoria (genuine food in an authentic setting); The King Wah, Victoria and the Ty-Foo, La Plaine (both are simpler in style than the "Mandarin" but the food served is well-thought-of).

French
The Swiss Restaurant, La Louise La Scala, Bel Ombre. Both offer ambitious French dishes (and sometimes Creole, too). The Swiss Restaurant looks out over Victoria.

Italian
The Baobab Pizzaria (situated on Beau Vallon beach); La Tartaruga Felice Mont Fleuri (looks out over Victoria's harbour.)

Others:
The Lobster Pot, Pointe Conan. Mussels and seafood prepared à la Creole or to suit the "international" palate. Sona Mahal, Anse Etoile, has the best Indian food on the island. Kyoto, Anse Etoile, offers authentic Japanese dishes.

ABC of the Islands and Beaches

There are about 100 islands listed by name, but to rattle them all off or describe them would be of little value to the holidaymaker, and only about a quarter of this number would, anyway, be suitable for a visit – however long or short. And even these need to be seen from the point of view of their suitability for "holidaymaking". Some would be nice to visit, but offer no accommodation or regular access routes, others may only be visited for scientific purposes and still others are in private hands and therefore "off limits" to the tourist.

As the Seychellois themselves differentiate between the "inner islands" and the "outer islands", so does this travel guide, and apart from giving pride of place to the main island of Mahé, the islands in each category are listed in alphabetical order. The granite islands and the two coral islands (Bird and Denis), which rise up from the Seychelles Bank, that massive underwater plateau, comprise the first group; these are also those islands which, normally, are the main holiday islands. The "outer islands" are those situated off the Seychelles Bank, in the deep waters of the Indian Ocean: the coral islands of the Amirantes, the Farquhar and the Aldabra group. These islands are so off the beaten track that one would not, in the normal course of a holiday, visit them, and therefore the descriptions have been kept brief.

The names of most beaches include the title "anse", a French word used to describe a bay – which will give you an idea of what most of them are like: exceptions apart, most are relatively small and gently curved. Those on the granite islands are backed by bizarre cliff formations and almost all are lined with tropical trees, such as palms, takamaka or casuarien. The beaches are, undoubtedly, first class: fine, light-coloured to white sand; pollution (apart from that caused by tourists), is unknown. The same goes for the sea: clear and clean, though in some places (e. g. Beau Vallon Bay) the water can sometimes be a little clouded by sand being stirred up due to high winds and a heavy sea.

Some Seychelles beaches have been criticized for being home to "sand fleas". Well, it would be nearer the mark to talk of "sand flies", which do appear in some places at certain times of the year and under certain weather conditions (none of the locals cann tell you when to expect them, though). Anyhow, some people seem to attract the little blighters and others they don't touch; the bites you get are not harmful, just irritatingly itchy. Insect sprays etc. are effective against them (Autan is one) and laying a blanket down on the sand, to sit on, helps too.

Reference to beaches is included with the description of the islands on which you will find them, in order to avoid confusion arising from the fact that some beaches, on different islands, have the same name: Grande Anse you will find not only on Mahé, but also on Praslin and La Digue.

Inner Islands

Mahé will likely be the first bit of Seychelles ground you touch, insofar as it is the only island with an international airport or harbour for ocean-going vessels. It is the principal island of the Seychelles, has the capital of Victoria on it and is quite unique amongst the islands of the archipelago.

✦ About 88% of the Seychelles population live here.

✦ The capital city, Victoria, with its 25,000 inhabitants (of the total of approx 64,000) is the largest urban area of the Seychelles.

✦ Most of the Seychelles' hotels are located on Mahé, and they represent about 85% of the total (Seychelles) bed capacity.

✦ Mahé, with its mountainous interior – the Morne mountains reach well over 1,900 ft., and the highest peak, Morne Seychellois, reaches 3,000 ft. – offers the most variety and contrast in terms of terrain and vegetation, ranging from exotic beaches to tropical mountain forests.

✦ Mahé has the best network of roads.

✦ Mahé has most of everything to offer the holidaymaker, from sport to entertainment and excursions – because of its importance and location, it is the "traffic junction" of the region, and offers the best opportunities for "island hopping" to the various other islands.

<u>North Mahé</u> is characterized by a gently sloping coastal strip on the east coast, and a hilly west coast which, in parts, has sheer cliff faces dropping down into the sea, and numerous little bays. It leads into the bay of Beau Vallon, the most important part of the coast for tourists.

<u>Central Mahé</u> – with the Morne Seychellois peak – is commanded from the east by the capital city of Victoria and its group of offshore islands, Ste. Anne, Moyenne, Cerf, Round and Long Island; the western coast is extremely rough and even inaccessible in parts.

<u>South Mahé</u> is the flatter part of the island, although there are some heights reaching to about 1,500 ft. The many bays in this area are pretty much unspoilt and are off the beaten tourist track.

Further information on <u>excursions and tours</u> on Mahé is given in the chapter "Out and About, In and On the Seychelles". Additionally, if it's of interest, in the botanical gardens you not only get a good insight into the Seychelles flora (including examples of the famed coco-de-mer),

Victoria, with its population of 15,000 (25,000 if we include the suburbs) is proud to be known as the "smallest capital in the world."

The centre is small and, therefore, ideal for the visitor. Everything which determines the character and appeal of the town is to be found within about a quarter of a mile of the "Clock Tower" ("L'Horloge").

On the streets which converge upon the "Clock Tower" you'll find good, reasonably-priced shops (esp. on Independance Avenue and in Victoria House.) Most banks, travel agents and airlines have premises in the area, too – as does the post office and the town's museum (in the Carnegie Library).

The Seychellois usually shop on Market Street – mainly because of the lively and colourful market (held on Saturdays) and the Indian shops which sell just about everything.

Also to be found in this part of town are the most "photogenic" of the old houses.

If you make sure you get to the Portuguese-style Capuchin House and the Cathedral of the Immaculate Conception (with the bell-tower behind it) in the north, to the old harbour in the east and to the botanical gardens in the south, then you will automatically have seen the most important sights Victoria has to offer.

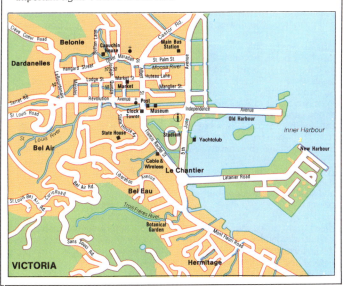

but there's also an enclosure for giant tortoises and the "Bel Eau" orchid garden with its approx. 150 species of orchids – in a natural environment – is worth taking a peek at.
<u>68 beaches on Mahé</u> means that it's difficult to make up your mind about which one to get to first. The main ones are:

<u>Beau Vallon</u> is the best-known of Mahés beaches. It offers the best and most varied selection of both accomodation (incl. 3 hotels) and water sports, including windsurfing, sailing and water skiing, the latter being mainly practised during the period May to November, when wind and water conditions are most suitable.

The mountains nearby overlook the 2-mile crescent of white sandy beach which is lined with takamara and palm trees. (North-west coast.)

<u>Grande Anse</u> is only a little over a mile long; hotels are situated close to, but not at the beach and it has fewer visitors. The lively sea makes for good surfing conditions – best from November to April – but strong currents might prove a hazard for the unaccomplished swimmer. The beach has more takamaka trees than palms. (South-west coast.)

<u>Anse à La Mouche</u> is a narrow, palm-lined bay; the waters are calm, and shallow at low tide. (South-west coast.)

<u>Baie Lazare,</u> called thus after Lazare Picault, who landed on Mahé with the first expedition, in 1742, is also a narrow bay and is protected by an imposing outcrop of granite. Good snorkelling, lots of shady trees. (South-west coast.)

<u>Anse Takamaka</u> has more palms to offer than its name would suggest, has a rather steeply-sloping beach. The occasional currents and hing seas occur mainly from May to October. (South-west coast.)

<u>Anse Intendance and Police Bay.</u> One is long and wide, the other a bit smaller, but both ideal Seychelles beaches with their granite cliff backgrounds; Anse Intendance has hundreds of palm trees and is secluded; Police Bay is one of Mahé's loneliest beaches, and photographs well because of the impressive surf.

<u>Anse Royal</u> is one of the east coast's longest beaches (about 2 miles long); good snorkelling from coast to reef. You can watch the local fishermen going out in the mornings, then landing their catch in the evenings.

Aride Island is the most northerly of the granite islands, lying about 30 miles north of Mahé and 10 miles north of Praslin. Its highest point is about 500 ft above the beautifully clear sea, and it is partly surrounded by a coral reef. Its isolated location, and its status as a nature reserve have allowed the largest colony of seabirds within the region of the granite islands to establish itself here. Nowhere else in the world can you see such large numbers of the roseate tern or the common noddy; both the greater frigate bird and red-tailed tropic bird nest here too. The great variety of plant life is worthy of note, and includes Wright's gardenia or bois citron, a bush with white blossoms. When the south-east trade winds blow, the island can only be landed on with difficulty because of high seas, and so days trips to the island are restricted to between October and April. The local travel agencies can arrange tours. Sailing times: from Mahé – 2 hours; from Praslin – 45 minutes.

Bird Island is the inner islands' other bird island of note, but quite different: the flat palm-covered coral island (privately owned) lies some 70 miles north of Mahé and can be reached by 'plane in about 40 minutes. Fairy terns and the common noddy are present in large quantities, and you also find the Madagascar fody, the peewits and the barred ground dove; the most amazing natural spectacle, however, is presented by the flight of the sooty terns which arrive here in their millions during April/May, and stay to breed and rear their young during October/November.

The island's special little zoological attraction, is the presence of two giant tortoises, of which "Esmeralda", at 150 years of age, is surely the world's largest, heaviest and oldest living example.

The white coral beaches are ideal spots for swimming, snorkelling and collecting shells; some way off the island, the seabed (Seychelles Bank) drops down vertically into the 6,000 ft. depths of the Indian Ocean proper, and the area is thus just the ticket for the deep-sea fisher.

Day excursions can be arranged from Mahé; the highly-recommended extended visits (several days) can also be booked in advance, from your local travel agent at home.

The occasionally used, old name for the island, "Ile aux Vache Marine", also alludes to the now evidently extinct "sea cow".

Cerf Island belongs to the Ste. Anne Marine National Park, and lies about 3 miles east of Mahé. This little island is covered in lush green vegetation, and several families eke out their existence on it, courtesy of the fruit and vegetables they plant and the coconuts they harvest and sell. A pretty restaurant here is well-known for its great Creole cuisine and is the target for lunch-time boat excursions to the "Park".

Zoological attractions: several giant tortoises and large colonies of the flying fox.

Cousin Island could be called "Mecca", if ornithologists and bird lovers had their way. It was purchased in 1968, by the International Council for Bird Preservation, as a haven for endangered species of land and sea birds. The brush warbler has found a last refuge here, and the Seychelles fody, the Seychelles turtle dove, the white-tailed tropic bird, the wedge-tailed shearwater as well as several types of terns, are indigenous to the island. The mind-boggling sight of thousands upon thousands of nesting sea birds awaits the visitor who comes here in April/May. The birds' well-being at heart, parties are restricted to 20 persons and are conducted only on Tuesdays, Fridays and Saturdays.

Trips are frequently ex-Praslin, but can be arranged ex-Mahé. Unfavourable wind or tide conditions can make passage through the reef difficult.

Cousine Island, Cousin's sister island, is in private hands; not accessible to the general public.

Curieuse Island is separated from Praslin by a sea channel just over a mile in width, and was, in the past, steered well-clear of – it having been a leper colony. The leprosarium was closed down in 1965, and the ruins of it and of the surrounding buildings can be visited. Only a maintenance man and his family now inhabit the island. Named after the island, the Curieuse Marine National Park's underwater flora and fauna differs from and supplements that of Ste. Anne's. The Indian Ocean Fishing Club, Grande Anse, Praslin, arranges visits.

Denis Island just like its close neighbour, Bird – is a coral island situated on the edge of the Seychelles Bank, privately owned and 50 miles distant from Mahé which can be reached in 35 minutes by air. Some parts of the island are densely wooded with palm trees, tamakas and casuarien trees, whilst other parts have been given over to the cultivation of produce to cater for the needs of guests staying in the bungalow village. (Only visits lasting several days can be booked; also in advance, at your home travel agency.) Lots of opportunities for sport – windsurfing, snorkeling, sailing and, particularly, deep-sea angling – lend Dennis the holiday island, that atmosphere of 'nature unspoilt'. Several Seychellois families and a number of giant tortoises live here permanently, whilst the odd turtle comes on land to lay eggs.

Frégate Island, the most easterly of the granite ones, 35 miles from Mahé, was once a renowned (notorious?), pirate's stronghold, but is today known and coveted rather for the ample and varied selection of plant and animal life it supports, its (up to 400 ft. high) hills and plateaux, woods, beaches and ease of access as exemplified – much to the benefit of the day tripper – by the convenience of a 25 minute flight connection to Mahé. Many come here especially to observe the great number of different land and sea birds, amongst which the magpie robin is a particular favourite: it loves this island above all others (hasn't been observed anywhere else, for a long time); since the island's owner had the "Plantation House" built in 1973, these birds are often to be seen in the vicinity of it.

La Digue, though not isolated geographically, enjoys the atmosphere and life-style of the most secluded of the inner islands. Only a few motor vehicles necessary for the transport of the basic needs of the population of approx. 2,000 inhabitants will be seen; main form of generally available transport is the oxcart or bicycle. The island as a whole gives the impression of being one great big palm grove with lanes along which many of the old type of plan-

Local islander's dwelling on La Digue

ters' dwellings still exist. It still has a traditional copra mill and a reserve has been established for the express benefit of the black paradise flycatcher which is known only to nest on this island. Unusual cliff formations can be seen along much of the coastline as well as in the interior, where they reach a height of up to 1,100 ft., and the beaches of many of the both large and small bays are also artistically framed by them, to a greater or lesser extent. Together with the colossal rocks, either freestanding or heaped on top of one another, they make up the archetypal picture of a Seychelles beach scene.

This applies particularly to the south-east of the island; to <u>Grande Anse, Petit Anse</u> and <u>Anse Cocos;</u> high seas and dangerous currents indicate caution when swimming. <u>Anse La Réunion,</u> the longest beach, is well-protected by a coral reef but during April to October you might be troubled by the vegetable matter growing in the water. <u>Anse Patate,</u> in the north, can be counted one of the most beautiful beachscapes; high waves break onto the white sand and against the rugged pink granite cliffs. The shallow waters of <u>Anse Gaulettes, Anse Grosse Roche</u> and <u>Anse Banane</u> provide good swimming and snorkeling up to the reef. Good snorkeling and diving is, however, to be had on the other side of the reef as well – as indeed in the waters around the island generally; the underwater seascape, including the base of the cliffs, is astounding. Refer also to: "Underwater Sports in the Seychelles".

All the beaches on La Digue can easily be reached by bicycle from the few hotels and guesthouses situated on the west coast.

Long Island, which is part of the Ste. Anne Marine National Park, is off-limits to the general public.

Moyenne Island also belongs to the Ste. Anne Marine National Park and looks nicely tropical and lush. It's a private island and has a restaurant which caters for parties of tourists and boasts an adequately-marked hiking path.

North Island, situated about 20 miles north-west of Mahé and 3 miles north of Silhouette, is a rock island; max. height 700 ft.; inhabitants do a bit of farming; day trips to here, are usually from Port Glaud.

Praslin has approx. 4,500 inhabitants who earn their daily bread mainly through fishing and/or agricultural labours, is about 7 miles long and 5 miles wide and, next to Mahé, is the archipelago's second largest island. The island is dominated by several mountain ranges which, in the west reach an altitude of 1,100 ft. or so, and, in the east, include the Vallée de Mai "National Park", the last home of the fabled coco-de-mer. (This botanical rarity is referred to frequently on the pages of this guide, e. g. under "Highlights", in "The Local Fauna and Flora", and in the chapter "Coco-de-Mer, the Fruit that Came out of the Sea."

If you have selected Mahé (25 miles away, as the crow flies) as your holiday base, you'll have little trouble getting here – and you must visit. The boat trip takes only 2 hours, the air "hop" will be a mere 15 minutes and the local tour and travel agents offer package tours even.

And, you know, you'd find Praslin a really smashing place to stay on, not just for a few days. You could possibly combine it with a stay on Mahé. The beaches vary in size and are not all that frequented.

The beaches on the west coast, if mostly fairly narrow, extend over miles, reaching from Anse Kerlan, via the bay of Grand' Anse, past Anse Bateau and Anse Takamaka to the southernmost tip of the island, Pte. Cocos. As there are only a few hotels or bungalows in Grand' Anse, the beaches will be more or less deserted most of the time. The east coast hotels, bungalows and guest houses are fairly widely spaced out along the somewhat shorter, but beautifully wide Anse Volbert beach, also called Côte d'Or. The best sailing, windsurfing and snorkeling conditions are yours for the asking here. Another thing that the above mentioned east and west coast beaches have in common is the fact that they all slope gently into shallow water which remains shallow, all the way up to the relatively distant reef.

Northern Praslin's jewel, acclaimed by connoisseurs as the most beautiful amongst granite beaches of the Seychelles – Anse Lazio may, despite its out-of-the-way location, be visited. You either walk, or cycle (very popular on Praslin) along the narrow track (from Anse Boudin), uphill and down dale, until you get there. The course may be a bit strenuous, but worth it.

Right at the other end of Praslin, at the top of the hill overlooking Pte. Cabris – is where the culinary art has reached its zenith on the Seychelles. That is the opinion of gourmets and the exclusive Chateau de Fenilles is where personalities dine in highly salubrious surroundings, to celebrate the delicate and fine à la Seychelles culinary "wizardry" of the man who is also maitre of the "Le Duc" restaurants in Paris and Geneva – Paul Minchelli.

Round Island exists twice as a small, flat green island in the Ste. Anne Marine National Park, and also as a bizarre tower-like configuration of granite, south-east of Praslin. Common to both is the good snorkeling to be had in the adjacent waters.

Sainte Anne Island, off Victoria, largest island in the Marine National Park which also carries its name, highest point the 800 ft. high Mount Ste. Anne, is privately owned and not normally open to tourists. It was one of the first of Lazare Picault's discoveries, in 1742, and although it was the white settler's first encampment after 1770, it was vacated after only a few short years.

Silhouette Island, is the third largest of the granite islands, lies about 12 miles north-west of Mahé and its silhouette is a well-known and impressive sight to those who, from Beau Vallon, have watched the sun sink into the sea behind it. It is a relatively mountainous island, the 2,400 ft. peak is named Mont Plaisir and the higher elevations are covered by an almost awe-inspiring old jungle which is home to a lot of rare trees. The 250 people who live here cultivate the coastal land, raising coconuts, cinnamon, sugar cane, tropical fruit and vegetables. Still to be seen here are a sugar cane mill and an oil mill, as well as a big old wooden colonial-style planter's house. The island has no streets, only pathways and tracks. The beaches, and the reef which has only a small gap for in-coming boats, are ideal for swimming and snorkelling. Day trips ex-Mahé.

Thérèse Island lies off the west coast of Mahé, is a small island with a relatively high elevation of some 500 ft. and some exceptionally good snorkeling beaches. Looking down from above, or from the boat if you're around on an excursion, you can see the giant "steps" of Pte. L'Escalier. One isn't quite sure as to whether they are to be attributed to nature, or to the Polynesians who began to settle Madagascar some 200 years B.C. Whole-day tours ex-Mahé; mini-tours possible too, from Port Glaud.

Outer Islands

The approximately 60 coral islands of the Seychelles (excluding Bird and Denis island) are dotted about in the Indian Ocean, some 700 or so miles to the south-west of the main island group. And some of them are nearer to either Africa or Madagascar, than to Mahé. A total of close on 400 people inhabit these islands – i. e. less than 1% of the Seychelles population. More to the point, most of them are uninhabited (the atolls are often no more than a shallow lagoon encircled by a strip of land which just about lifts itself up – a few feet – above sea level). The number of islands which are anything like productive, in the economic sense of the word, is very small indeed. Some islands serve as either temporary or permanent bases for scientific study.

The island of Cöetivy lies directly south of Mahé, is unique in this, but is not accessible. Apart from this exception to the rule, the outer islands (to which Cöetivy counts) can basically be viewed as comprising the following island groups: the Amirantes, the Farquhar group and the Aldabra group.

The Amirantes are closer to Mahé than all the other groups, lying between 120 and 200 miles distant from it. The inhabited islands are Alphonse, Daros, Desroches, Marie Louise and Poivre, and only half of these possess a landing strip: Desroches, Marie Louise and Daros. Most of the islands are visited regularly every two to three months by the M. S. "Cinq Juin", on which matters of, and people on business (workers, officials and the like) are the "priority" cargo. Visits of a private (tourist) nature should be cleared with the owners of the respective islands (most are privately owned). The owner of Poivre, for instance, is a German chap who offers a good programme of water sports, including diving and deep-sea angling.

The Amirante's economically most significant island is **Desroches,** about 150 miles from Mahé; the copracup from here is considered the best in the Indian Ocean. During the breeding season (April to September) **Desnoeufs** is home to hundreds of thousands of terns.

The first humans to set foot on these islands were, presumably, Arabs, back in the 9th century AD, but they received their name in 1501, from Vasco da Gama who rediscovered these islands on his second journey to India: Illhas do Almirante (Admiral Islands).

Farquhar was also discovered by a Portugese seafarer: Juan Nova. 1504 is when he called. The islands of the group – Farquhar, Cerf, St. Pierre and Providence – lie variously at between 430 and 500 miles from Mahé.

Farquhars hook-like shape hugs one of the Indian Ocean's most beautiful lagoons. Skippers like to put in here because it is always con-

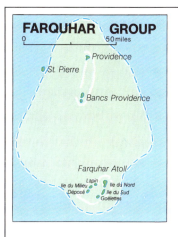

veniently accessible. "Twenty Five Franc" Beach is renowned for its splendour: over a mile long with sand as fine as flour, the beach slopes gently into the warm and shallow turquoise sea. The island's economy is based on copra production and fishing; lots of palms and casuarien trees give the island a nice "finish". The island of Goëlette, in the southernmost atoll, is a haven for migratory birds, principally the terns. The atoll's northern island has had an airstrip for a number of years now.

Aldabra, the main island of the group which also features **Cosmoledo, Assumption** and **Astove,** has certainly made as much of a name for itself as any of the other islands of the archipelago. It was the centre of much controversy during the 60's, when it had been planned to establish a military base here, which would have sounded the death knell for this unique atoll and the giant tortoises it supports. However, the island found unexpected friends and champions in the right quarters, and the enemy was finally routed, in 1967: no base. The island was declared a nature reserve, under the administration of the "Seychelles Island Foundation", whose patron is the President of the Seychelles M. Albert René. Since a research station was established on Picard (west), there's been nothing but natural history research work going on in Aldabra.

See also the chapter "Aldabra, Galapagos of the Indian Ocean".

Cosmoledo and the island of Astove are over 600 miles from Mahé, and Aldabra and Assumption nearer 700. But for that Aldabra is only 400 miles from the Tanzanian coast and about 250 miles from Madagascar! One credits the Arabs with having landed here first, in the 10th century A.D. "Al Khadra" was what they called it, and the Portugese made that into Al Hadara – and in time it ended up as Aldabra.

Cosmoledo is of a similar geological construction to Aldabra. It has a large variety of indigenous sea birds, especially boobys, and one finds relatively large numbers of turtles in the waters around the island.

Assumption used to be a bird island at one time, but the birds changed their idea of where their breeding places should be, changed

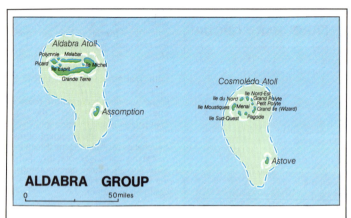

islands and, voilà, in 1840 the thousands of years worth of deposits (droppings) was turned into a commercially valuable asset: guano. So far, over a million tons of this natural manure have been excavated and it represents a not inconsiderable entry in the annual export balance sheet. The traditional market for this product has been Mauritius, where it has played a positive role in the cultivation of sugar cane.

Farquhar and Astove (Aldabra group) have an airstrip each, so far, but most goods, and passengers, still arrive by sea (as in the case of the Amirantes). The "Cinq Juin" services the more important of the two southerly groups every two to three months, from Mahé. One could also, of course, charter a schooner any time. For further details see also under "Useful Information".

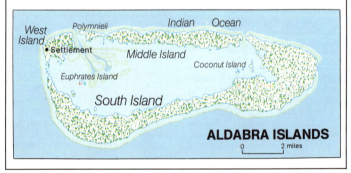

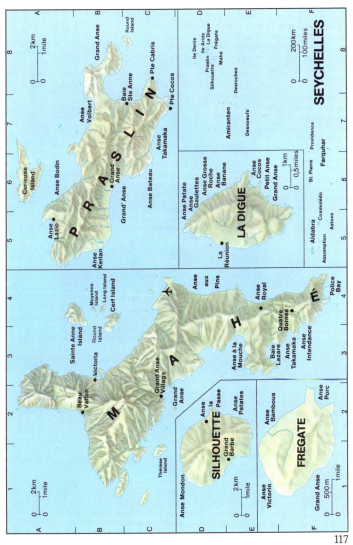

Seychelles

The following denominations are currently in use:

Notes: Rupees 10, 25, 50, 100
Coins: Cents   1, 5, 10, 25
        Rupees 1, 5

Useful Information

Currency
The Seychelles rupee is the official currency.
1 rupee = 100 cents.
(For current exchange rates see enclosed fold-out map.)

Exchange Control Regulations
Unlimited amounts of the rupee may be either imported or exported. You will, however, not find many banks (outside of the Seychelles) which offer them.

Foreign exchange is, similarly, not restricted – neither import nor export, but export thereof may not exceed the amount originally imported – for which reason it's a good idea to declare same if you are carrying large amounts (of currency) part of which you may wish to re-export.

Changing Money
You get a better rate (in rupees) for your currency, in the Seychelles. So it is advisable to buy them there.

The hotels can change money for you, but the banks offer the most advantageous rates. International air passengers could indeed take advantage of the facilities for changing money at the airport – to purchase your first batch, or to change back any rupees you still have left at the end of your holiday.

The exchange rates given by the banks are laid down by the government and are published in the daily newspaper, "Nation".

Travellers' Cheques, Credit Cards
Travellers' cheques quoted in any of the European currencies, as well as in US$ can be changed at banks and hotels, the banks offering the better rate; not all shops are equipped to cash them. The same applies to credit cards, and even some of the car hire companies (especially the locally-based firms), do not accept credit cards as payment. The hotels which are frequented by visitors from overseas do, however, accept this form of payment, and American Express, Diner's Club and Visa are accepted names. Eurocheques are, so far, only accepted by the banks.

Entry Formalities
You need only a valid passport to gain entry – applies equally to nationals of any country. Entry is normally granted for a period of four weeks, but may be extended, in the country, should you wish to prolong and are able, on demand, to produce evidence of having sufficient funds.

Vaccination/Immunization Requirements
Nothing in force, unless you have come from a country or area in which there is an epidemic (officially declared infested area), in which case the respective certificates of health must be carried.

In Case of Ilness
Victoria has a well-equipped hospital

and there are several smaller clinics in the administrative area of Mahé and on Praslin and La Digue. In emergencies, whether illness or accident, treatment is within the framework of the (Seychelles) National Health Service; basic fee SR 75. Medicines are dispensed in the hospital pharmacy or in either of the two chemist shops (pharmacies) in Victoria. It is advisable to take any regularly required medicines along with you, frome home.

Sickness and accident insurance is something you should invest in before going in holiday. Your travel agent, amongst others, can advise you.

Hints on Health
Protect yourself well against sunburn, especially in those first days of your holiday; you must take care, even on overcast days and when there is a cooling breeze.

A high protection-factor sun cream, sunglasses and something to cover your head are called for. You should even wear a T-shirt whilst snorkelling. Depending upon tidal conditions, sea urchins may be washed up on some beaches — wear sandals or similar. You won't have much luck trying to get one of these spines out of your flesh yourself. As with cuts and grazes from sharp coral, disinfect the wound thoroughly to avoid infection and a spoilt holiday. Sea urchin spines are absorbed by the body in time; local home-remedies to speed up this process include vinegar poultices, rubbing lemon juice into the affected area, or hot wax applications. If in doubt, consult a doctor.

You need have no reservations about eating any of the fruit or salads, and you can drink the water too — although you may well prefer to drink from the jugs or carafes provided by room service.

Gnats and the like are not normally a problem (monsoon, air conditioning). If necessary, the hotel will provide insect sprays.

Should you discover any lizard-sized geckos on the walls or ceiling of your room, don't worry: try not to frighten them away; they are perfectly harmless and help to keep insects and flies down.

Languages
Creole, once a dialect with many French elements in it, is now the official language. The languages of instuction are English and French; Englis' is a fairly safe bet for communication with the populace. If you speak French as well — all the better.

Car Hire
In addition to the chapter "Out and About, in and on the Seychelles", here now some facts and figures about current charges for hire cars. One can rent various cars, from a Mini to larger Japanese models. Prices for unlimited mileage range from SR 250 to SR 270 daily, or SR 230–250 for 3 to 6 days. In case of an accident you would have to pay at least the first SR 2,500 (excess) of any claim, unless you pay an extra SR 40 daily, or SR 240 per week for comprehensive cover. The charges are subject, additionally, to a 5 % tax. Petrol is extra and costs

quite a bit more than in Central Europe (1 litre cost about SR 4.97 at the end of 88). When you pick up your vehicle, check how much petrol is in it; it often happens that cars are hired out with only about ¼ of a tankful of petrol! As there are only 5 petrol stations on Mahé, it might prove tiresome being stranded somewhere, out of gas. These stations are in Beau Vallon, Victoria, across the airport, Anse Royal and Seychelles Sheraton (7am–3pm). Drivers must be 21 years old; national driving license is sufficient and no upper age limit applies.

Most hire companies can also provide chauffeurs at an extra charge of SR 75 per hour or 500 SR (based on a 8 hour day) per day.

The most popular vehicle is the Mini Moke, a sort of jeep-like, open-topped affair. Daily rate SR 250–280; weekly about SR 230–270 per day.

In the period December 15th to January 15th you should make your hire car bookings well in advance, i. e. from home, when booking your holiday.

Bicycle Hire
On Praslin and La Digue one can hire out bicycles which, however, are not exactly cheap. The lowest price (if hired for several days) is about SR 25 daily, but it can often be as high as SR 30 to SR 40 for a single day.

Traffic Regulations
You drive on the left. Speed limit is 40 mph. on Mahé. 25 mph. on Praslin. In Victoria, and indeed in all built up areas, 25 mph. is your top speed.

Taxis
Taxis do not have meters. The prices for hirings, from either Victoria to the airport, or from the hotels to the more important and popular places of interest, are officially laid down. The taxi driver is required to carry a copy of the charges for these routes with him at all times; your hotel is fully informed of the price structure too. Ask at your hotel what the price for a specific drive should be. Examples: airport to Reef Hotel, SR 25; airport to Beau Vallon Hotels, SR 70; airport to Barbarons Beach Hotel, SR 80; Victoria to Reef Hotel, SR 50; Victoria to Beau Vallon Bay Hotels, SR 30. The (empty) return journey is already included in the price, so if you go to an out-of-the-way place as, e. g. to a restaurant in southern Mahé, it will be cheaper (and more reliable) to pay the driver waiting time, than to pay for a second taxi to come out some hours later.

All the above prices apply to Mahé, between the hours of 6 a.m. to 8 p.m. Prices on Praslin will be about 20% higher. The night surcharge payable is not the same on both islands.

The cost of taking in the more popular round-trip excursion by taxi is only minimally higher than what car hire charges plus the extras come to. Do your best to negotiate a good price.

The main taxi rank in Victoria is opposite the Anglican church, behind the main Post office.

Public Bus Services

The S.P.T.C. bus routes cover pratically the whole road network on Mahé, and link the capital, Victoria, with the various hotels and villages. Read all about it in the chapter "Out and About, in and on the Seychelles". The buses are the principal means of transport available to the populace and fares, in keeping, are low: per mile, the bus fare is one tenth that of a taxi fare. For example: Victoria to the Reef Hotel costs 4 rupees. You don't get return tickets, as you only pay per stage, i.e. per bus stop travelled. The central bus station in Victoria is in Palm Street, opposite Unity House. On Praslin you still get some of the smaller lorries, with wooden seating fixed up on the back, used as buses.

Ferries and Ships

Regular ferry services operate, principally, to serve the needs of the local population; thus the ferries from Praslin and La Digue travel to Mahé in the mornings, and back from Mahé in the evenings, meaning that if you make use of them, you need to plan to be away for at least one night. You can, however, take advantage of day trips as offered by local tour operators/travel agents.

The ferries plying between Praslin and La Digue enable you to take ½ day trips to La Digue, also in combination with a flight "hop", Mahé – Praslin – Mahé. Package tours are offered by the local travel agents.

You can take a cruise on the government supply ship "Cinq Juin", on its runs to the Amirantes (12 days round-trip) or to Farquhar/Aldabra (20 days). Holidays for tourists are really only catered for on Poivre Island, one of the Amirantes group. The cruise costs SR 2,700 and the run alternates between the two destinations, every two to three months.

Ship and Boat Charter

Motor boats for either joyrides or deep-sea fishing excursions can be chartered from the "Marine Charter Association" at the harbour in Victoria, or from Beau Vallon Bay. Half day costs SR 1,500 to SR 2,000 whole day SR 1,600 to SR 2,500. A number of hotels on Mahé, Praslin, La Digue and Denis have their own boats, which they hire out.

Yachts and boats which can accommodate from two to ten people can also be chartered for outings lasting from one day to several weeks, including excursions as far as to Aldabra, or diving expeditions (all the necessary gear included). Marine Charter Association, and Gregoire, La Digue, can set you up. The rates vary from SR 2,400 to SR 7,000 per day per ship; you can book up and join in, on certain tours.

Diving Centres

Presently there are six well-equipped diving centres: Sheraton, Blue Lagoon Chalets, Northolme and Coral Strand in Mahe; La Réserve in Praslin and La Digue Island Lodge.

The centres are fully equipped to cater for up to 20 divers (10 litre air tanks, compressors, lead belts, weight-jackets and ABC). Experienced divers will have their own equipment.

Best time to do it, when underwater visibility is at its best, is: November to May, when the water is calmest. From May onwards the boats can sometimes have difficulty laying off because of high winds. Including the boat, going out diving would costs you about SR 135 per drive.

Air Traffic
With its new fleet of Twin Otter machines in service now, Air Seychelles operates regular daily flight services to Praslin, and a charter service to (amongst other destinations) Denis and Frégate. Praslin (also in combination with La Digue) and Bird Island "hops" are available as package tours from local travel agents.

Airport Charges
No taxes levied – whether for interisland or international arrivals or departures.

Postage, Telephone Charges
For example, via airmail to Europe: post card SR 2, letter (up to 10 g.) SR 3. The charge for an International Direct Dialing call to Europe is SR 29,26 per min. Hotels add a service charge (varies from hotel to hotel), but you can make calls direct from Cable and Wireless Ltd., in Francis Rachel Street, Victoria, should you so desire.

Hours of Business
Banks in Victoria are all usually open from Monday to Friday, 08:30 hrs. to 13:00 hrs.; their branch offices e. g. those in Beau Vallon, Anse Royal and at the airport open 09:00 hrs. to 12:00 hrs. A few banks also open during the afternoons and/or Saturdays: Habib Bank and Bank of Credit & Commerce Internationale – 14:30 hrs. to 16:30 hrs. The latter and the Banque Francaise Commercial also open Saturdays, from 08:30 hrs. and 09:00 hrs. respectively to 11:30. Banking hours (Barclays) on Praslin are: Ste. Anne, Monday to Friday 08:30 hrs. to 12:00 hrs.; Grand Anse during weekdays between 14:30 hrs. and 15:30 hrs.

The bank counters at the airport additionally open for business to coincide with each international flight arrival or departure.

Post office in Victoria: main post office, Mondays to Fridays from 08:00 hrs. to 16:00 hrs. On Saturdays it is open from 08:00 to till 12.:00 noon. Sub-Post offices are often to be found adjacent to the local police stations. Airmail post handed in at the main post office before midday, usually will leave on either the evening, or first plane next morning.

Shops open Monday to Friday from 08:00 hrs. to 17:00 hrs., some close for lunch between 12:00 noon and 13:00 hrs. Saturday times are 08:00 hrs. to 12:00 noon.

Victoria market is mostly a morning affair.

Mains Voltage
240 v. AC., most hotels have either European or English-style sockets.

Tipping

Most hotels and restaurants include a service charge in the bill. Where this is evidently not the case, add 10% if satisfied with the service; should a service charge already be included, a tip of between 3 and 5% is a nice gesture. Porters and the like receive 1 rupee from yourself per bag carried and you give the chambermaid 2–3 rupees per day of your stay.

Dress

Light, airy cotton clothing is most suitable; the sort of thing you'd wear for the beach. One or two long-sleeved shirts or pullovers can come in handy as protection against the sun, especially during the first days of your stay and for boat outings. The regulation "plastic mac" or similar protection against sudden hefty showers, will stand you in good stead. Whereas the ladies are often seen wearing long dresses or kaftans during the evenings, the gentlemen are not frequently be seen in formal dress.

It is not done to wander about town in beach wear. Topless bathing, on the hotel beaches, is tolerated (a concession to modern ways) though not encouraged; nudism is frowned upon to the extent of prohibition, but what you do on a lonely beach, where nobody can see you, is your business. When scampering about on the reefs, wear something on your feet to avoid cuts.

Where to Stay

There are 2,800 tourist "beds" available on the Seychelles. Most of this is hotel or guest house capacity, some is holiday bungalow accomodation and a few beds are available in private lodgings.

There are some 45 hotels on Mahé, Praslin has 9 and on La Digue there are another 4. The coral islands of Bird and Denis have one each. Hotels are also available on Desroches, Felicité (2), Frégate and Silhouette Islands. The Amirantes and Moyenne have all of 12 guest beds available. The guest house is a Seychelles speciality – most were formerly private houses; atmosphere and service is personal, and number of guests limited.

Cuisine offered is generally Creole.

Camping is not allowed on the Seychelles.

Holiday/Festivities Calendar

1/2 January	New Year
March/April	Good Friday, Easter
1st May	Labour Day
5th June	Liberation Day (parade)
	Corpus Christi
29th June	Independence Day, national youth sports festival
15th August	Assumption of Our Lady
September	La Fete La Digue, annual regatta
1st November	All Saint's Day (All Hallows)
November	Annual deep-sea fishing championship
8th December	Celebration of the Immaculate Conception
25th December	Christmas Day

Customs Regulations

To the Seychelles: in addition to your own personal effects, your tax-free allowance includes 200 cigarettes or 50 cigars or 250 g. tobacco, 1 litre of spirits, 1 litre of wine, 125 ccs. of perfume, 250 ccs. of toilet water as well as presents to a value not exceeding SR 400 in the case of adults, and SR 200 in the case of children under 18 years of age. The importation of weapons, (includes air guns), ammunition, harpoons and drugs is prohibited. Neither may you bring in seeds, plants, flowers, fruit, vegetables, tea, meat or meat products.

From the Seychelles: you can export (according to the Seychelles regulations) whichever of the island goods happen to appeal to you. If you want to take a coco-de-mer, you need to obtain an export certificate from one of the authorised dealers.

Information relating to customs regulations governing what you may or may not import into your own country (i. e. take home with you) and applicable tax-free allowances, can be obtained at the airport customs office; the airlines are helpful, or you could check before you leave home.

Diplomatic and Consular Offices

Any tourist information office or your travel agent will be able to let you know where your embassy or consulate is located; it's very useful to have the address and telephone number to hand, in case of loss, or damage to personal property or effects – or should you require repatriation!

Literature

The following publicatons, all of which are only available in the Seychelles, are recommended reading material:

1. Seychelles, from One Island to Another. By Claude Pavard
2. Flowers and Trees of the Seychelles. By Francis Friedmann, published in 1986.
3. Coco de Mer, the Romance of a Palm. By Guy Lionnet, published in 1986.

Information about the Seychelles

Please refer to your local travel agent or write to
Tourist Information
Independence House
Independence Avenue
<u>Victoria/Mahé</u>

*   *   *

Contents

Photographs

Impressions in pictures	6
Captions	34

Impressions

They Go by the Name of: The Seychellois	37
The Seychelles – And that Quip about the "1,000 Miles"	38
Mr. Grimshaw and the Ghosts of Moyenne	40
Highlights	41
Victoria, the World's smallest Capital	46
Michael Adams the Painter	48
Underwater Sports in the Seychelles	49
Coco-de-Mer, the Fruit that came out of the Sea	52
Aldabra, Galapagos of the Indian Ocean	54

Information

Historical Ups and Downs	56
☐ The Seychelles at a Glance	57
History of the Seychelles, at a Glance	58
Location and Formation	60
Climate, and when to go	62
The local Flora and Fauna	64
Fascinating Underwater World	73
The commercial Aspect	75
☐ There's Copra, and there's Copra	77
Tourism: Currency Earner and Problem Child No. 1	80
The Seychelles, the Gourmet and the Gourmand	82
Entertainment	86
Seychelles Rhythms	87
Out and About, in and on the Seychelles	88
What's That in "Creole"?	92
Sports . . . Sport	94
Souvenirs, Souvenirs . . .	98
Works of Art in Miniature	100
Photo Tips	101
Mahé's Restaurants in Brief	104
ABC of the Islands and Beaches	105
☐ Victoria	107
Map Victoria	107
Map Amirantes Group	114
Map Farquhar Group	115
Map Aldabra Group	116
Map Aldabra Islands	116
Map Seychelles	117
Money	118
Useful Information	119
Contents	126

Map

Please note:
Every effort was made to ensure that the information given was correct at the time of publication.

However, as it is not possible for any travel guide to keep abreast of all changes regarding passport formalities, rates of exchange, prices, etc., you are advised to contact the appropriate authorities (embassy, bank, tourist office...) when planning your holiday.

The publishers would be pleased to hear about any omissions or errors.